I0494656

"IF I WERE A CARPENTER"

ART EXHIBITION

JULY 2016

CURATED BY STEVEN R. FUJIMOTO

THE LOFT STUDIOS AND GALLERIES
401 SOUTH MESA STREET, 3RD FLOOR
SAN PEDRO, CA 90731

"If I Were A Carpenter"
Group Art Show from July 7, 2016 - July 30, 2016
Curated and Forward by Steven R. Fujimoto

CONTRIBUTORS
Book design by Ellen Riingen
Published by GreenieArts
Printed by CreateSpace

Image contributions by
Ellen Riingen
Ginger Van Hook
Hung Viet Nguyen
Marjan Vayghan
Steve R. Fujimoto
Karrie Ross
Marlene Picard
Kristine Schomaker

Cover artwork by Rachel Lauren Kaster

All rights reserved. No part of this book may be reproduced or transmitted in any form or by any means, electronic or mechanical, including photocopying, recording or by any othe information storage and retrieval system without written permission.

Copyright ©2016 GreenieArts, Steve R. Fujimoto

ISBN-13: 978-1535327879

SPECIAL THANKS TO:

Peggy and Ben Zask at

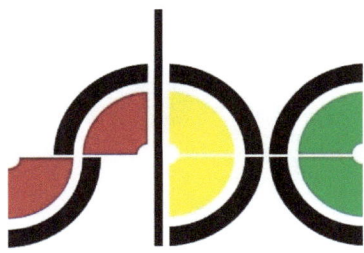

HTTP://SOUTHBAYCONTEMPORARY.ORG

and

Janice Lloyd Govaerts from

THE LOFT STUDIOS AND GALLERIES

401 SOUTH MESA STREET, 3RD FLOOR
SAN PEDRO, CA 90731

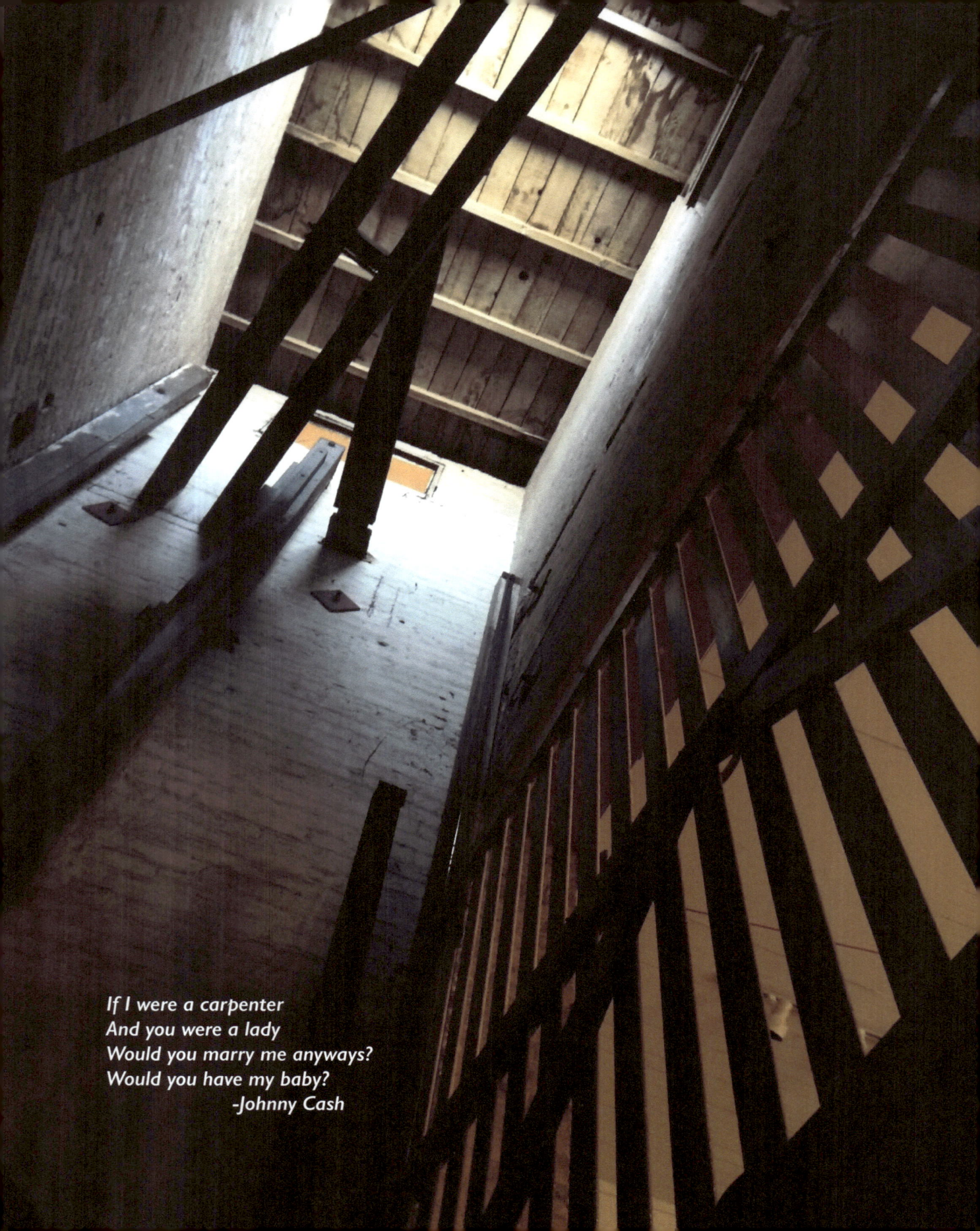

If I were a carpenter
And you were a lady
Would you marry me anyways?
Would you have my baby?
                    -Johnny Cash

TABLE OF CONTENTS

THE ARTISTS

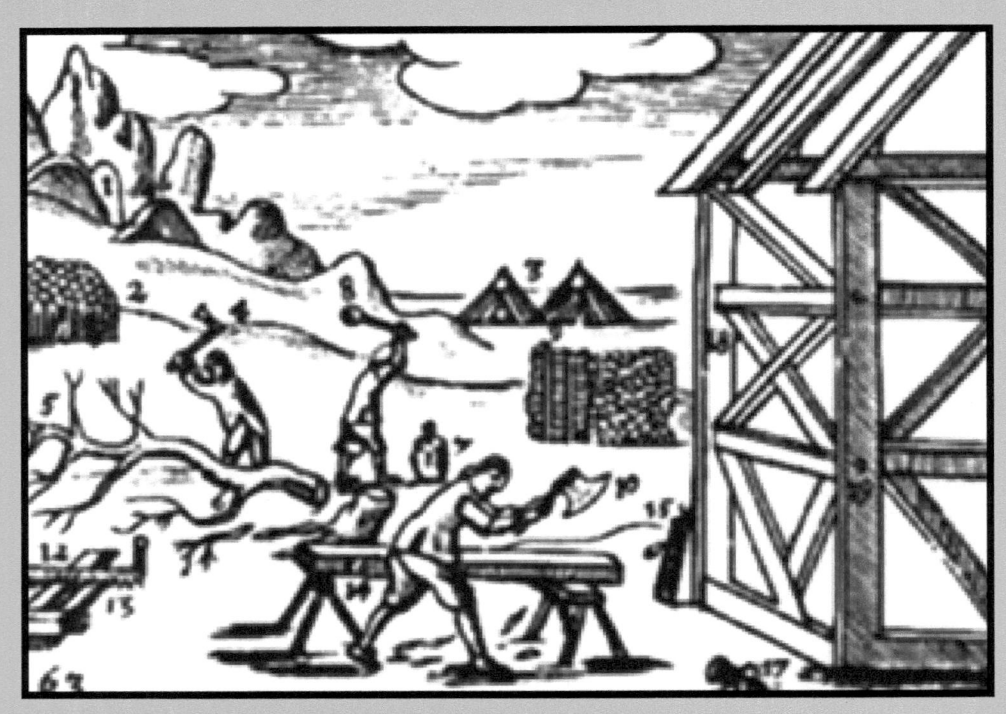

IF I WERE A CARPENTER . . . . .

FOREWARD

In researching the premise that artwork created using carpentry skills is a gender-neutral pursuit, I came across signs that at least one major institution formally recognizes that neutrality. From an early age, both boys and girls who participate in the Scouting program may acquire a carpentry merit badge by displaying similar levels of competency: Demonstrated ability to use craft tools in a safe manner, showing knowledge about careers in related fields, and creating a final project using the acquired skills.

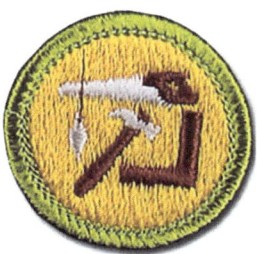
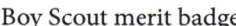
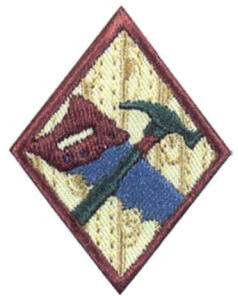

Boy Scout merit badge   Girl Scout merit badge

Given that within the Scouting community the opportunity to learn basic carpentry is offered to both genders, I was interested in exploring what parallels may exist in the art world -- and in particular, how artists might demonstrate the idea of neutrality in their artwork.

Since 1881, when The United Brotherhood of Carpenters and Joiners of America was formed, the percentage of women working in the field today is woefully small—less than 10%. Yet within the art world as suggested by the artists who participated in this show, the concept of neutrality and transparency was on full display.

On the day of drop-off, I found myself amazed by the depth and range of artworks as they arrived at the gallery. Every piece was unique in their subject matter, material, execution, and interpretation of the theme. The transparency and neutrality were remarkable. Materials and techniques were embraced by all with equal aplomb.

Artists have always been pioneers in defiance of the general norm. Those artists who participated in the exhibit, "If I Were a Carpenter" demonstrated that spirit with vigor and enthusiasm.

Steven R. Fujimoto
Curator/Artist

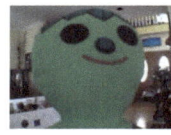

THE ARTISTS

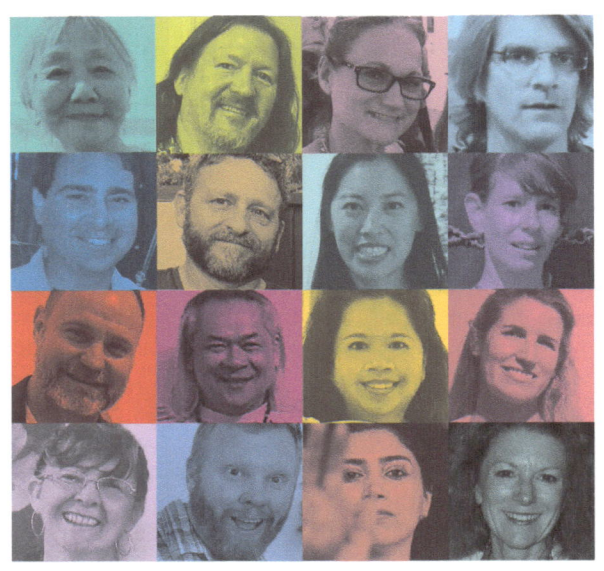

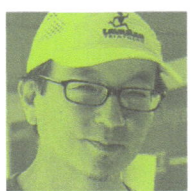

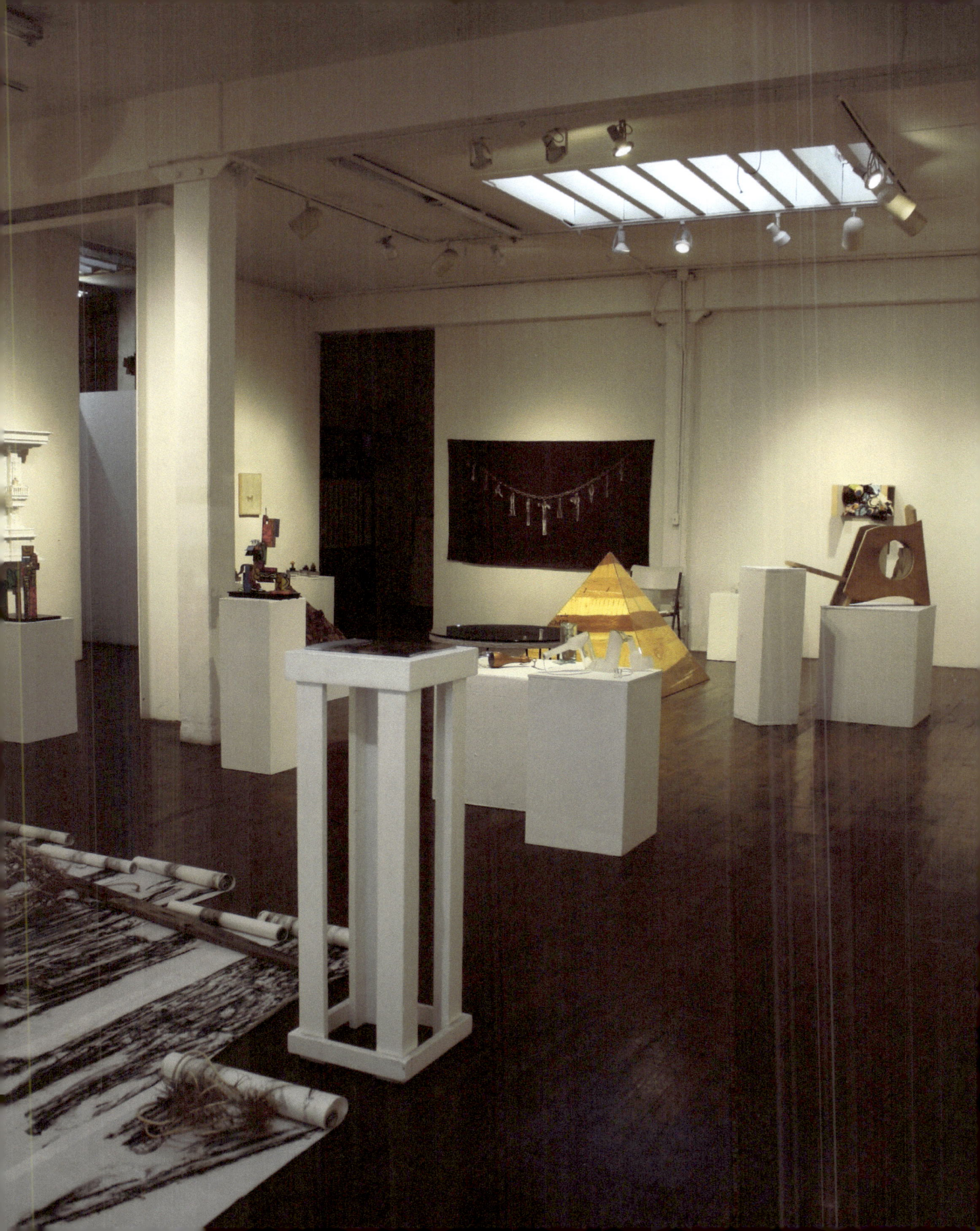

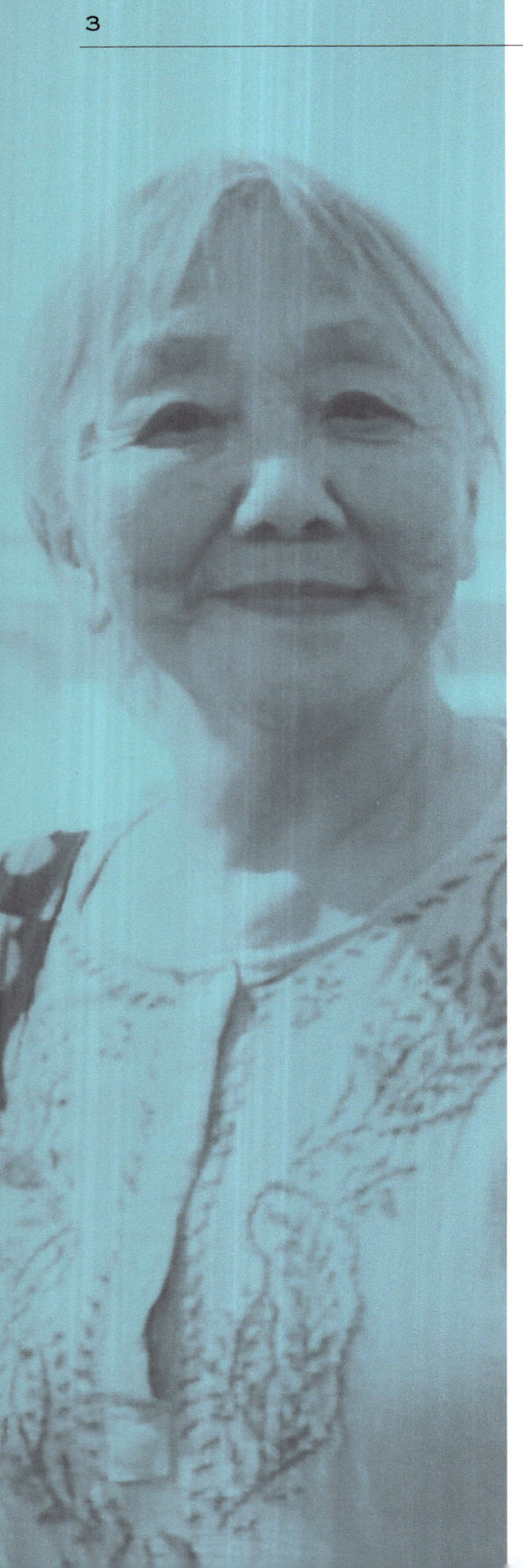

MARY BONIC

"The Spirit has no form, yet that which moves and transforms the form is the Spirit." - *Wang Wei AD 699-759*

The Spirit in me is far more powerfully knowing as it reveals itself through my creative expressions. I come to that conclusion because what is created is never something my conscious mind would ever have imagined or predicted on its own.

The internal and intuitive process, governed by the Spirit, remained the constant through the years, fueling my growth as an artist and providing me with increasing faith that the path I travel is the correct one for me. I continually seek the specifics in the visual world I am creating. It is created organically so it moves toward its own destiny and I follow its lead. It is a wondrous feeling, looking at a brand new living thing, world, place, being, that stands in its very own light of life, no longer mine.

MARY BONIC WAS BORN IN BUK TOY VILLAGE CHINA AND GREW UP IN HONOLULU, HAWAII. SHE RECEIVED HER BACHELOR OF SCIENCE DEGREE FROM BOSTON UNIVERSITY AND A MASTER OF FINE ARTS DEGREE FROM THE UNIVERSITY OF HAWAII. IN 1983, MARY MOVED TO LOS ANGELES AND IN 1989 MOVED INTO THE SANTA FE ART COLONY IN DOWNTOWN LOS ANGELES.

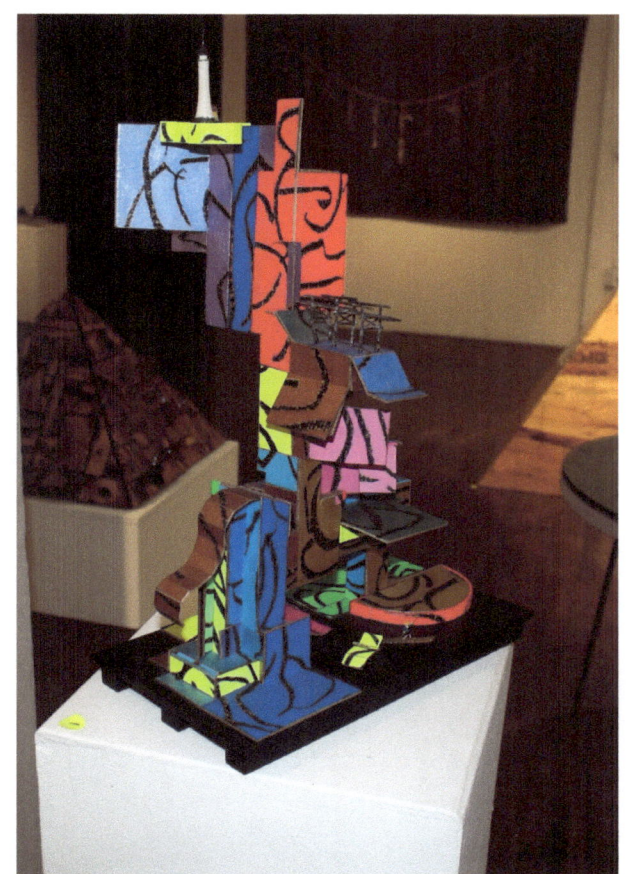

Title: "China On My Mind"
Medium: Mixed Media Sculpture
Dimensions: 7" x 12" x 16"

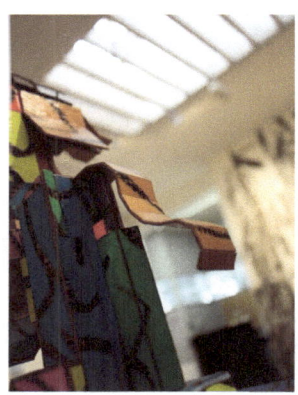
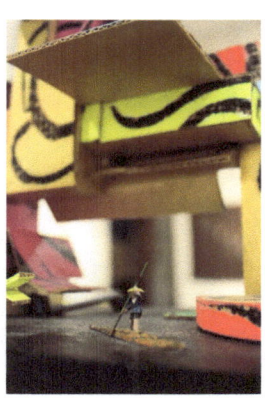
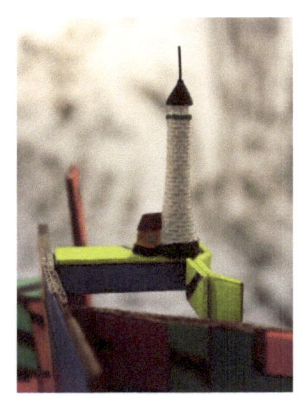
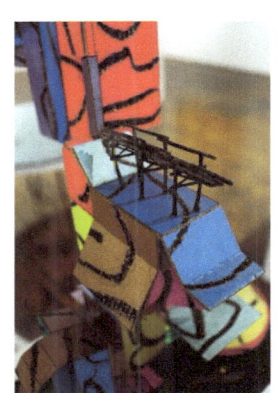

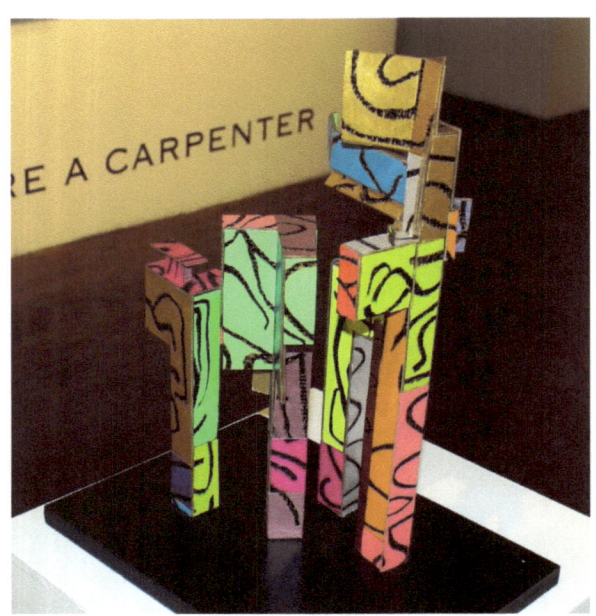

Title: "Ohana"
Medium: Mixed Media Sculpture
Dimensions: 8" x 13" x 16"

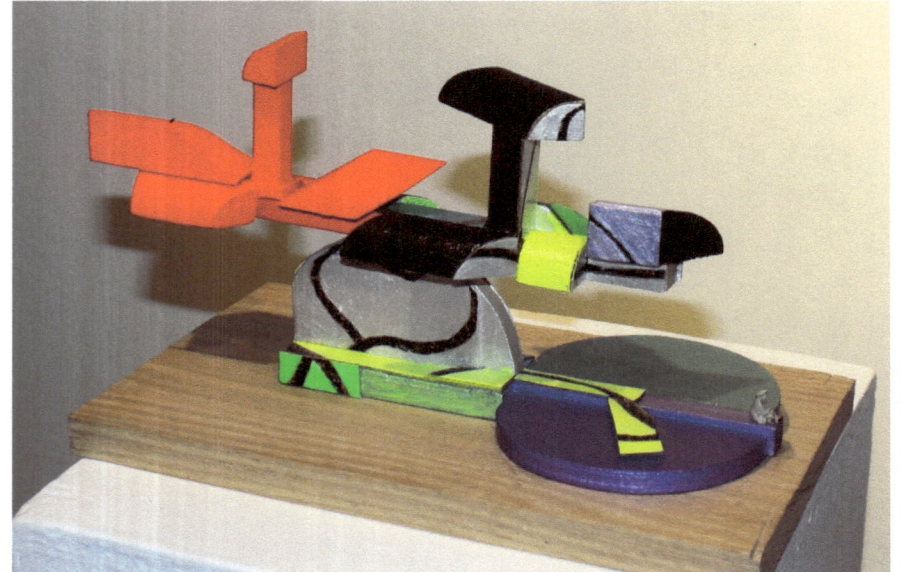

Title: "Into A New World"
Medium: Mixed Media Sculpture
Dimensions: 8" x 12" x 8"

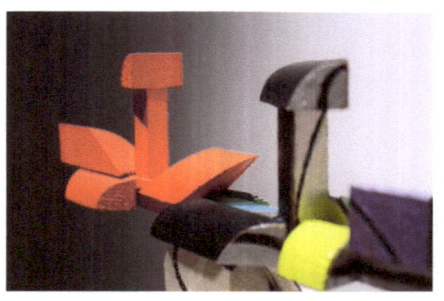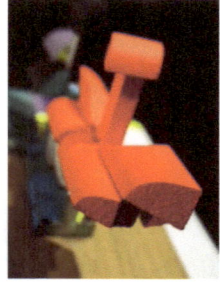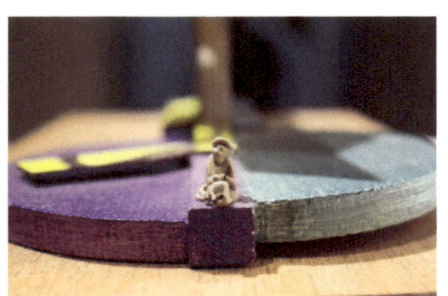

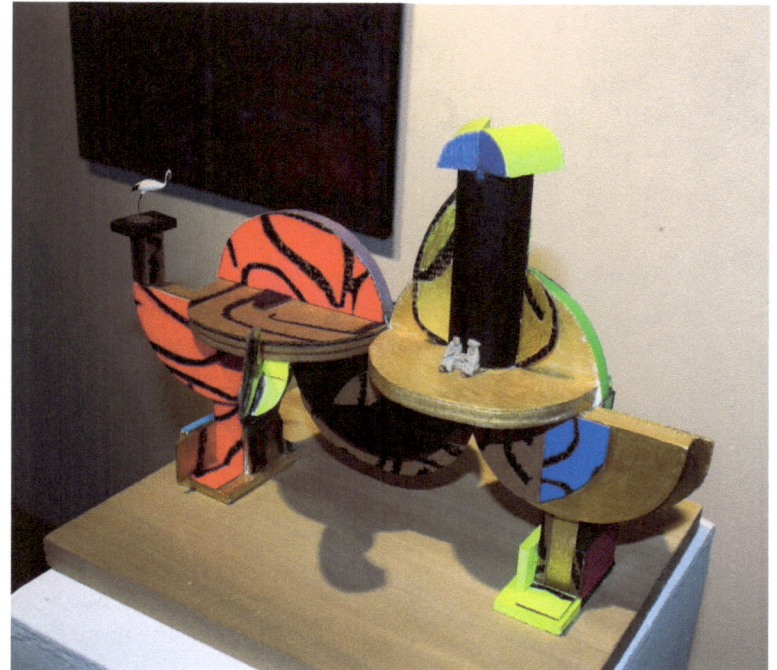

Title: "Island"
Medium: Mixed Media Sculpture
Dimensions: 8" x 10" x 8"

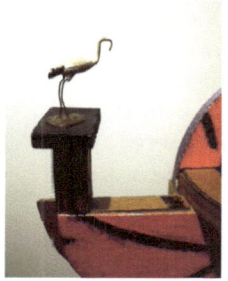
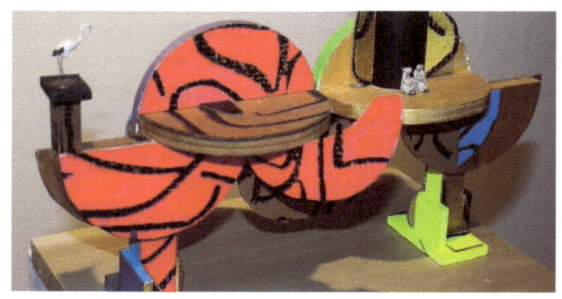
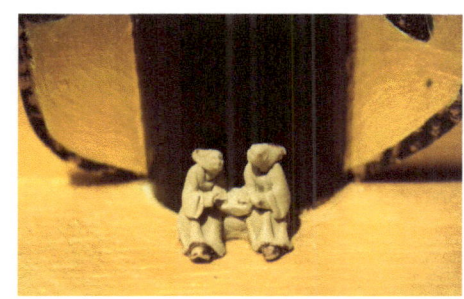

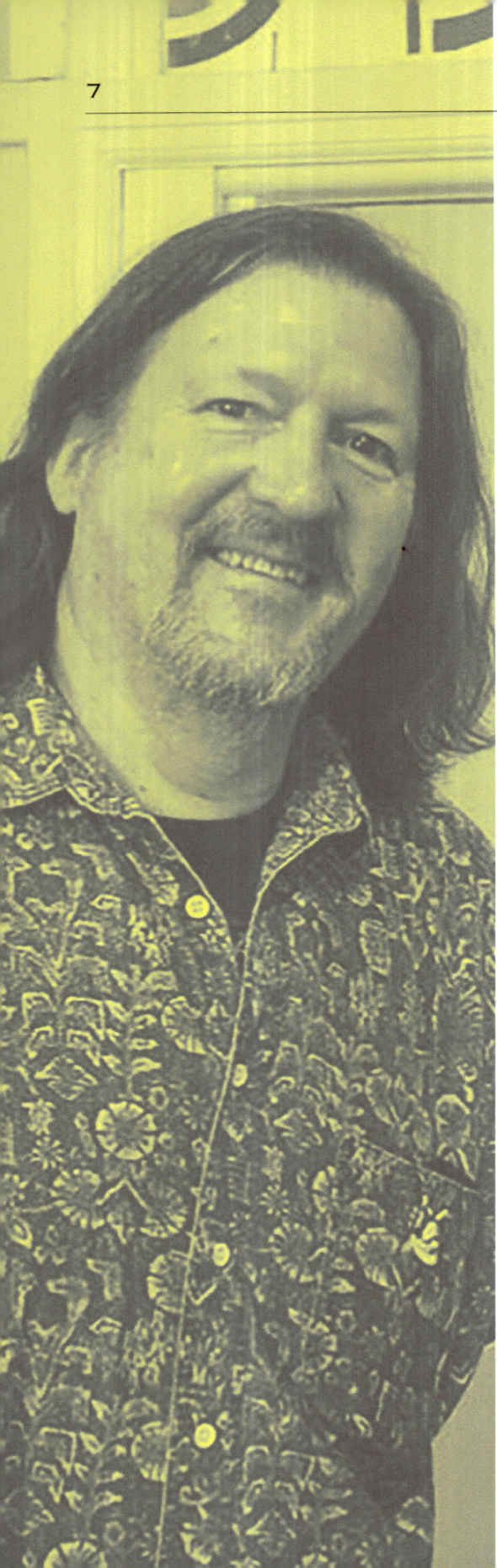

Michael
CHOMICK

As a figurative artist, I consider myself an engaged observer and the works are reflections addressing issues relevant to these times. My work maintains a strong focus on a singular theme - Exploration of the "Human Condition". This singular theme became apparent to me as I focused on developing my own artistic language and style from the early stages of my career as a fine artist, after an eleven year career as a commercial artist.

The works are statement-driven in an attempt to shed some light on issues of major concern that have been relegated to the shadows and systematically ignored. On occasion, I produce pieces with nothing more than a displayed sense of humor so as not to take myself too seriously.

Since the initial development of my art, I have always been interested in the wonderment and discovery of what drives behind all human nature and the societies to which they live. The genesis of the works, often stem from a point of inquiry that I wish to convey tangibly for the viewer so that they may pose a dialogue within themselves. This internal dialogue may result towards their own personal advancement, and growth as an individual, in turn a better society.

MICHAEL CHOMICK IS A VISUAL ARTIST WHOSE WORK HAS ENCOMPASSED MEDIUMS OF PRINTMAKING, MIXED MEDIA CLAY SCULPTURE, SMALL TO MURAL-SIZED OIL PAINTINGS, ACRYLIC/BAS-RELIEF PAINTINGS, INK OR GRAPHITE DRAWINGS, AND MIXED MEDIA CONSTRUCTIONS. FOR NEARLY 3 DECADES (1987-2016), HIS AWARD-WINNING WORK HAS BEEN EXHIBITED BOTH NATIONALLY AND INTERNATIONALLY.

WWW.MICHAELCHOMICK.COM

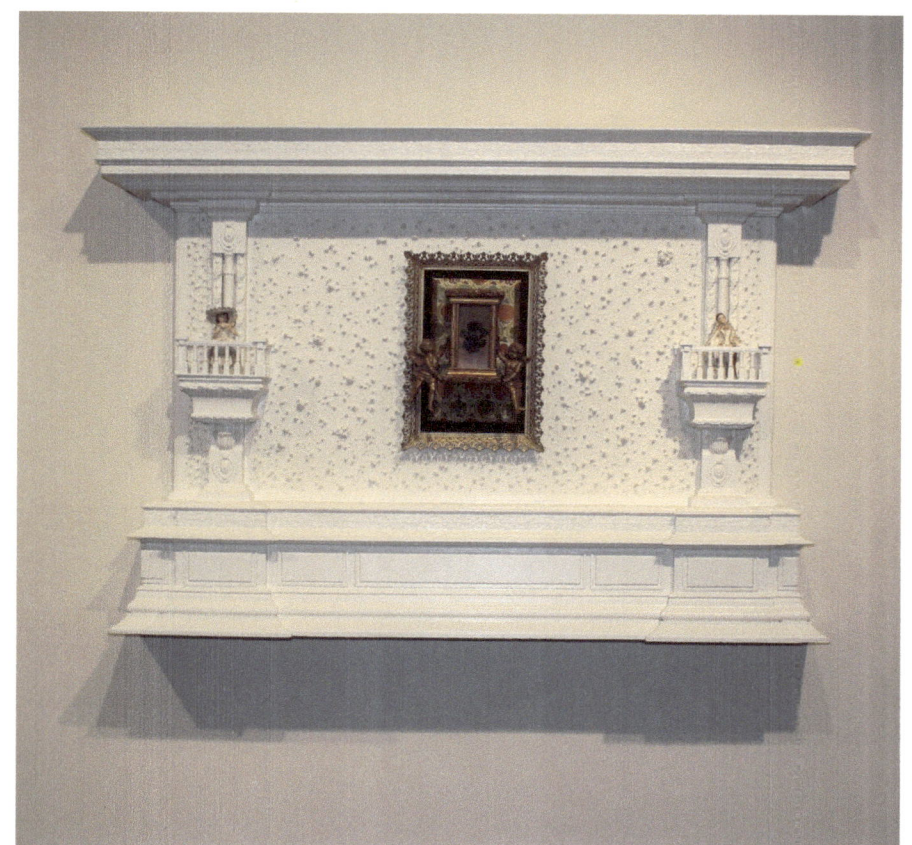

Title: "THE TRANSFIGURATION OF TEA"
Medium: Mixed Media Wall Sculpture (wood, ceramic figurines, resin figurines, fabric, gold ornate serving tray, black wrought iron leaf fragment, cebia thorns, latex paint)
Dimensions: 41"x 60" x 10"

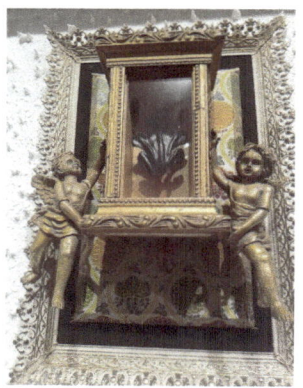 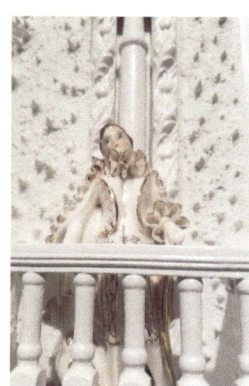 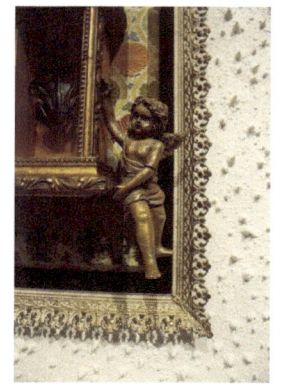 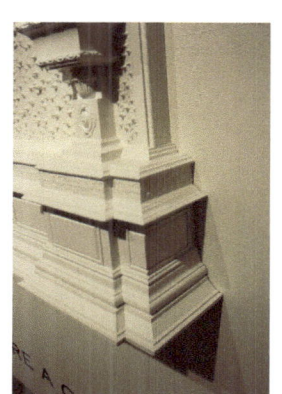

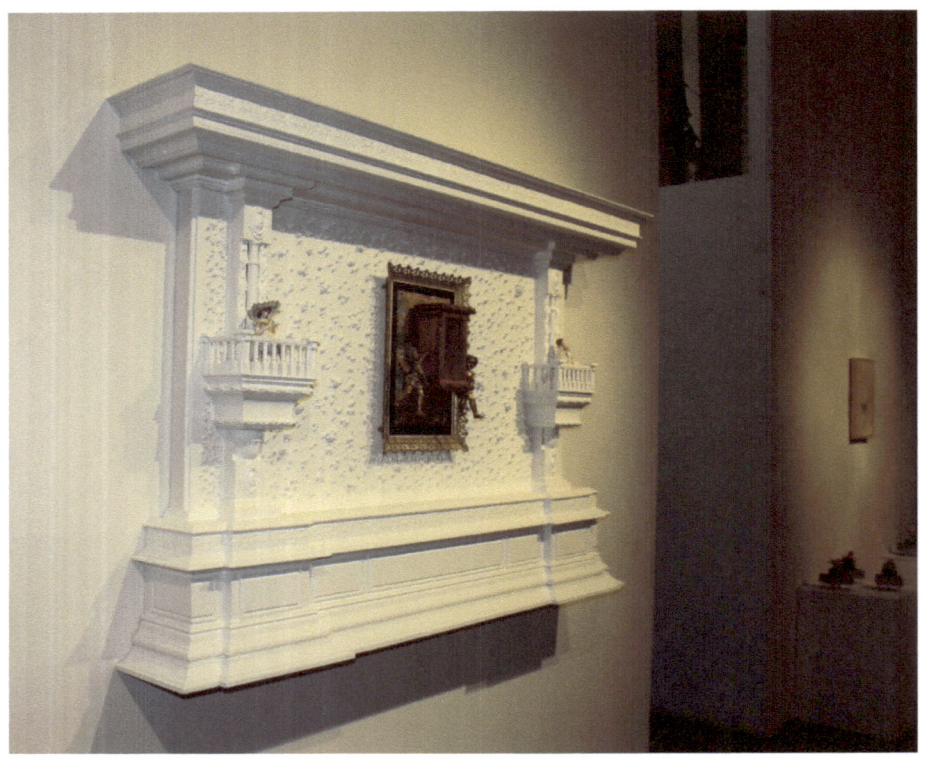

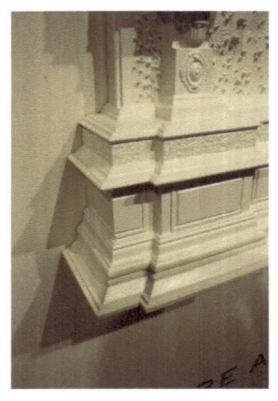 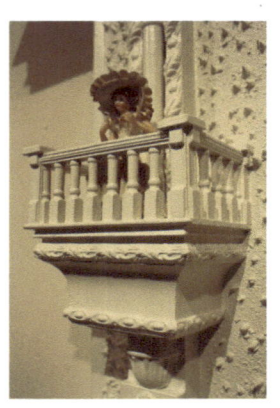 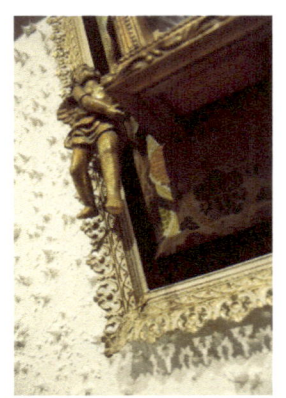 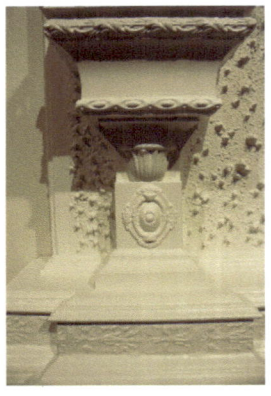

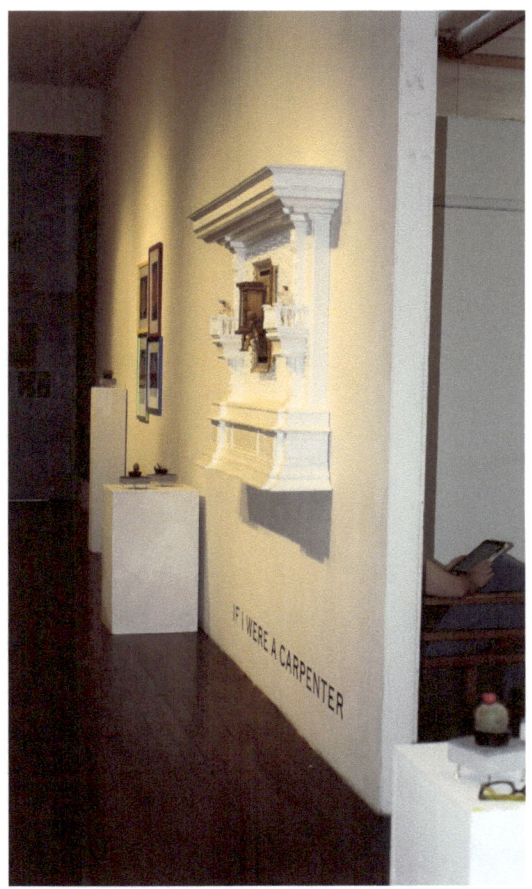

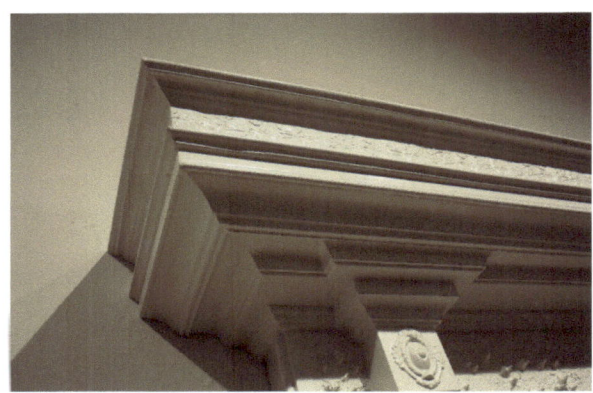

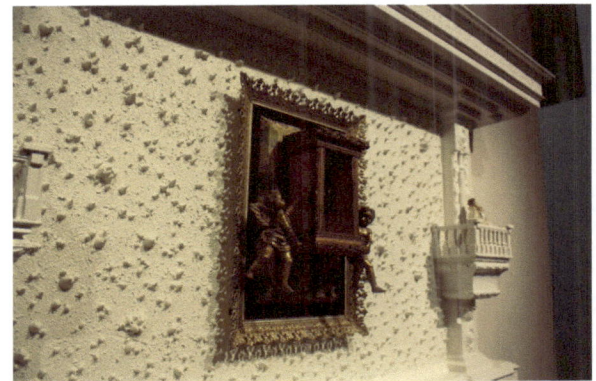

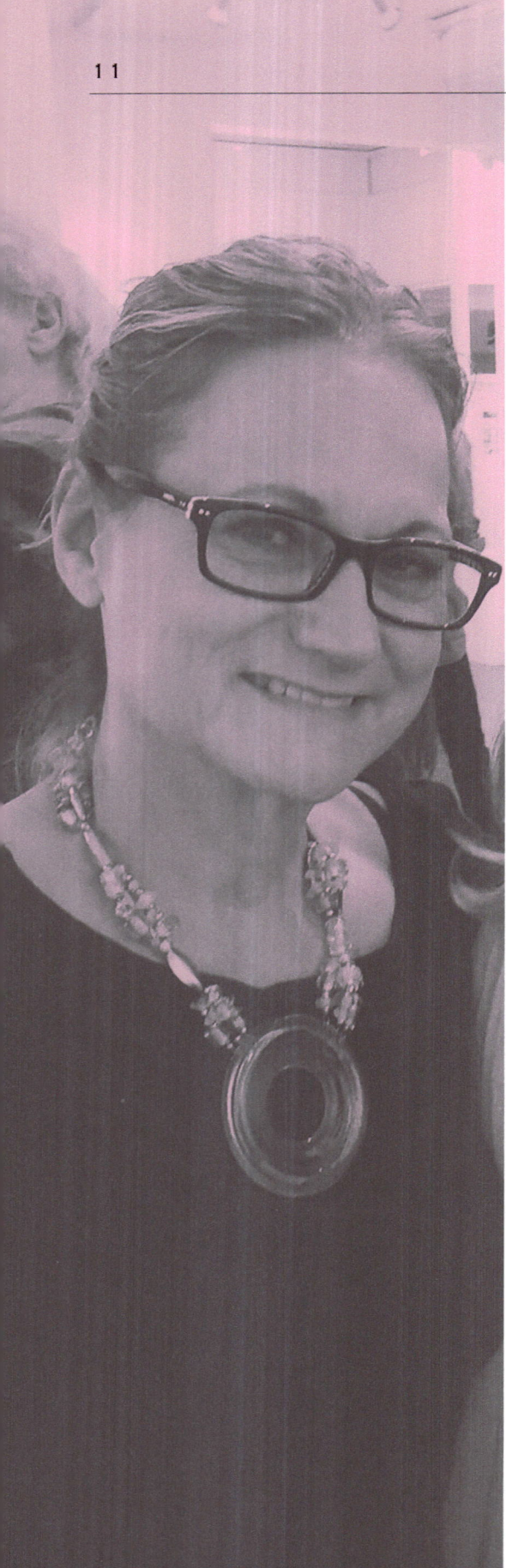

June
DIAMOND

June has created and exhibited an extensive body of work throughout the years. Hundreds of her pieces are held in private collections worldwide. She has taught stained glass and hot glass techniques privately in her studio and offsite for over twenty years.

June expanded her use of materials to include metals such as steel, copper, aluminum, and brass. Her work often involves the use of recycled materials such as glass and metal, manipulated through processes including welding, cutting, drilling, heating, and painting. She also creates large scale installation pieces and functional art.

JUNE DIAMOND HAS RECEIVED HER B.F.A FROM CALIFORNIA INSTITUTE OF THE ARTS. SHE CURRENTLY RESIDES AND MAINTAINS HER STUDIO IN SOUTHERN CALIFORNIA SPECIALIZING IN HER FASCINATION WITH GLASS.

HTTP://WWW.JUNEDIAMOND.COM

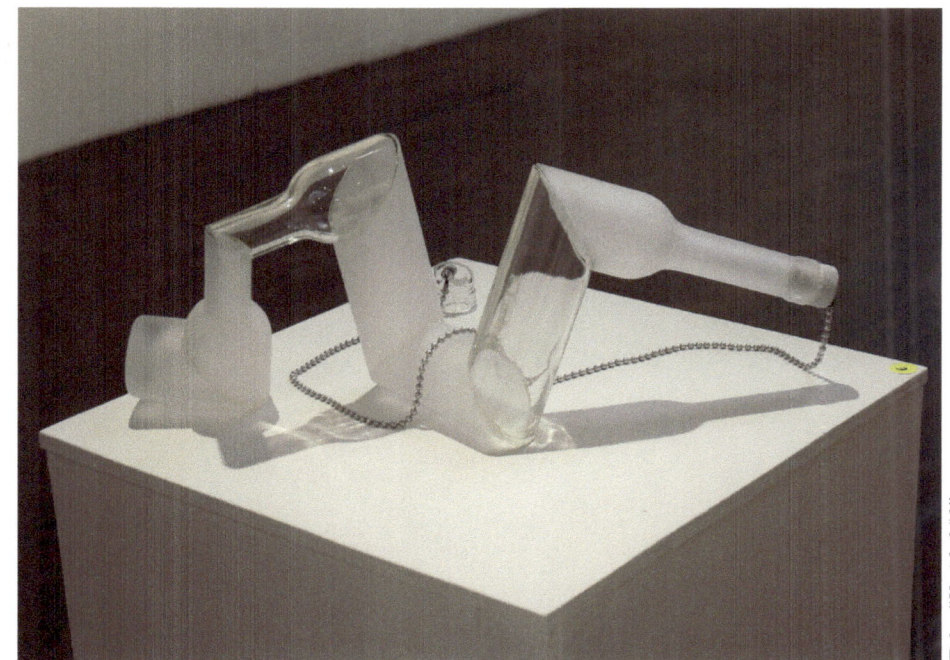

Title: "Untitled #1"
Medium: Cut/Frosted Glass, Lanyard
Dimensions: varies

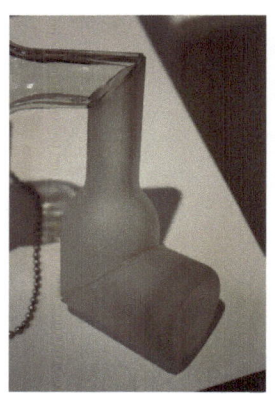
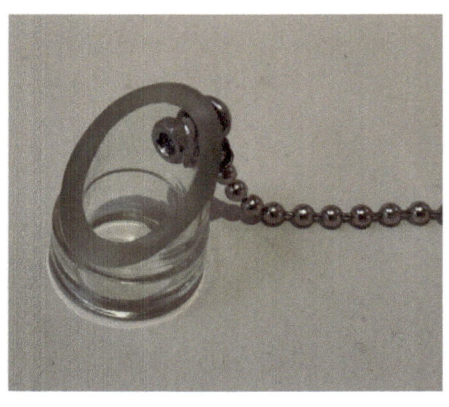
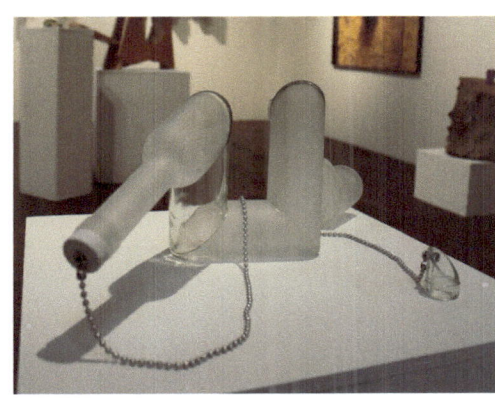

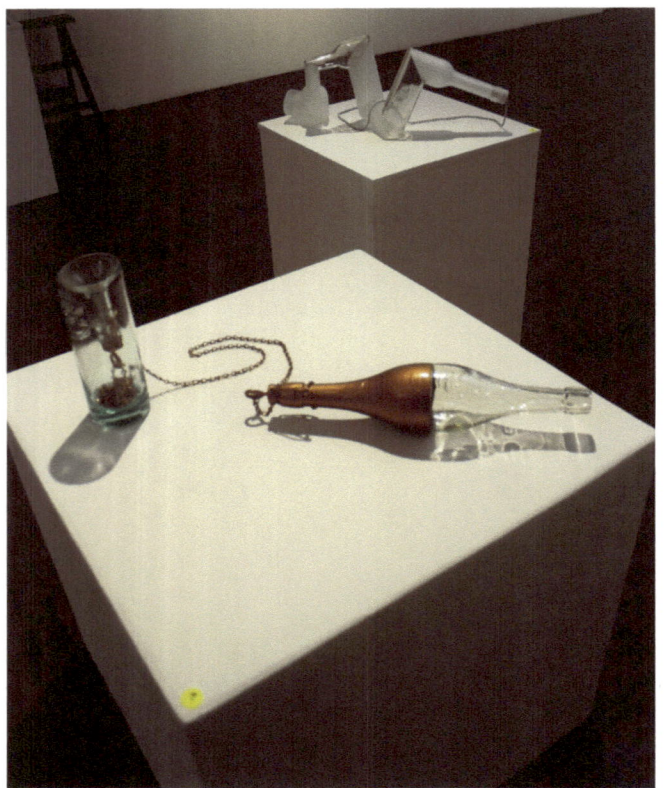

Title: "Untitled #2"
Medium: Cut Glass, Metallic Enamel, Chain
Dimensions: varies

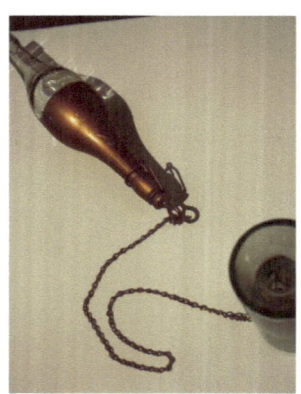 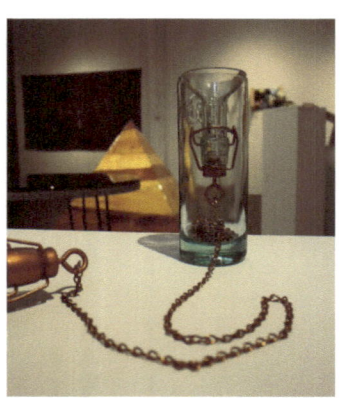 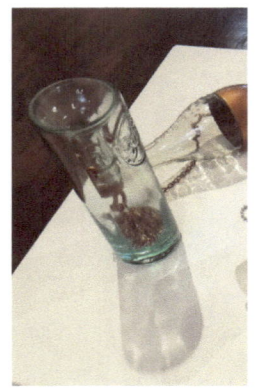 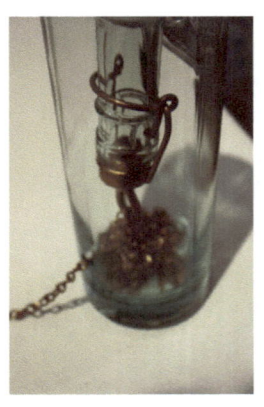

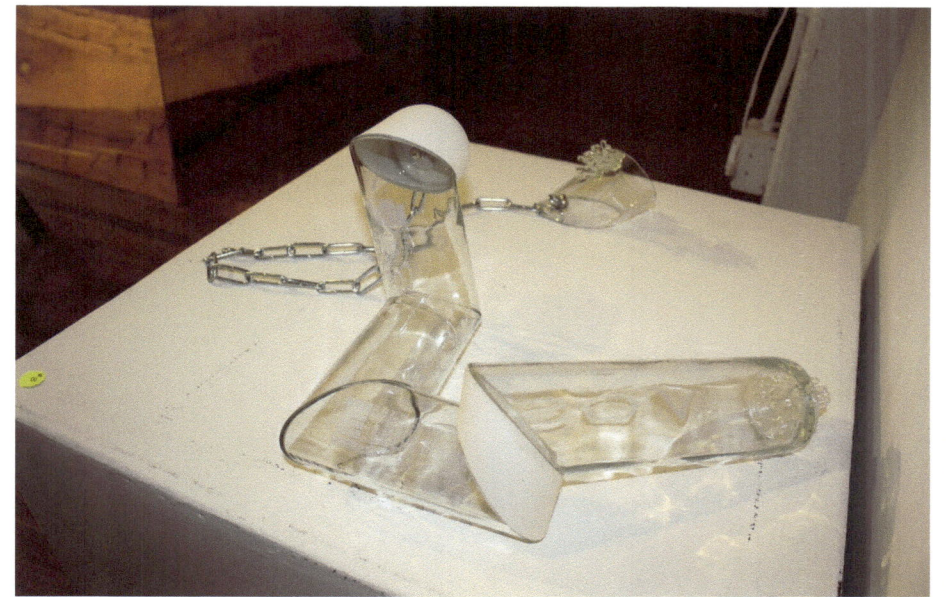

Title: "Untitled #3"
Medium: Cut Glass, Fused Glass, Chain
Dimensions: varies

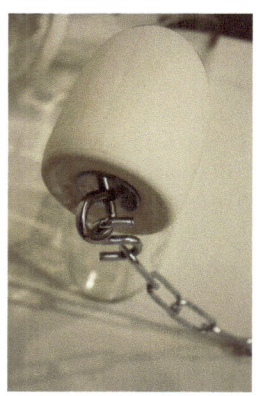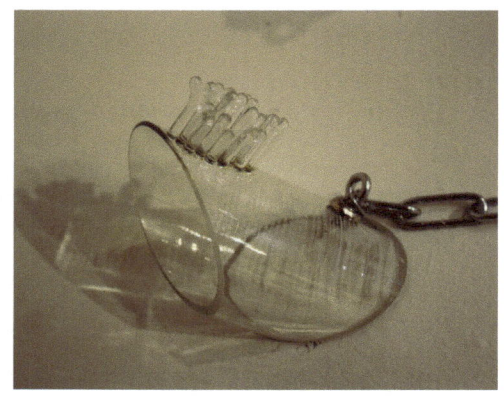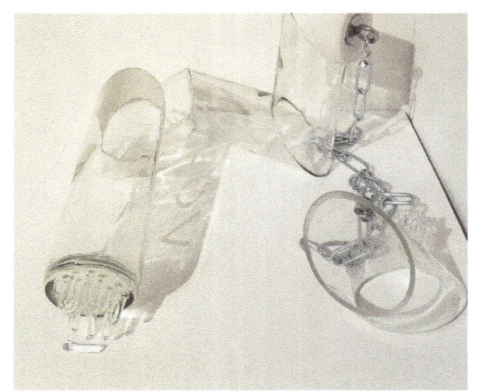

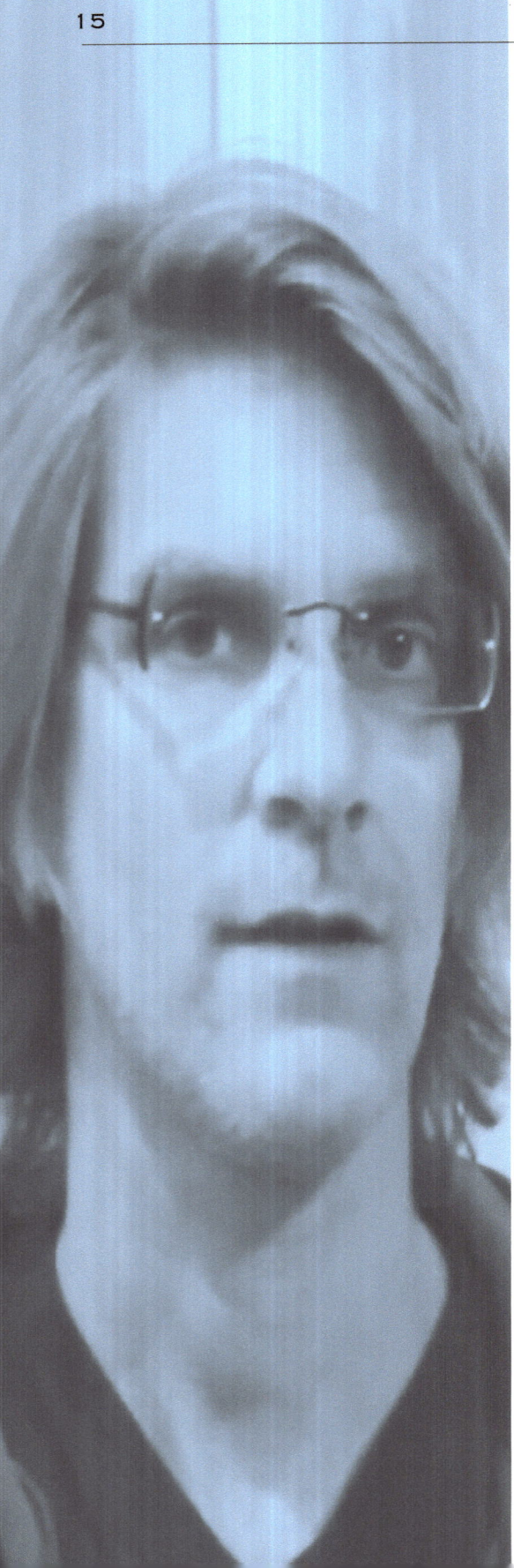

MARK X.
FARINA

"Work fast,
Cure slow,
Destroy before collecting dust."

-Mark

MARK X FARINA IS A MULTI-MEDIA POP ARTIST WORK-
ING IN VENICE, CALIFORNIA. SINCE HIS EDUCATION
IN EDINBORO UNIVERSITY AND OTIS COLLEGE OF ART
AND DESIGN, HE HAS GONE ON TO EXHIBIT THROUGH-
OUT NATIONWIDE.

HTTP://WWW.MXFARINA.COM/

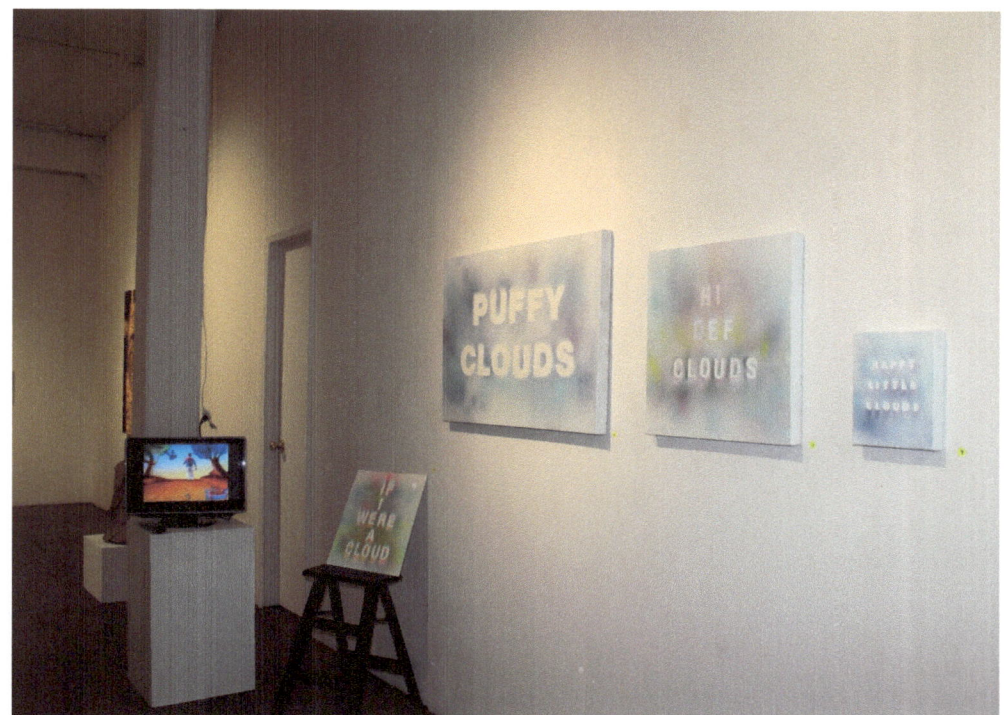

Title: "If I Were A Carpenter, I Would Build The Sky"
Medium: Video Manipulation

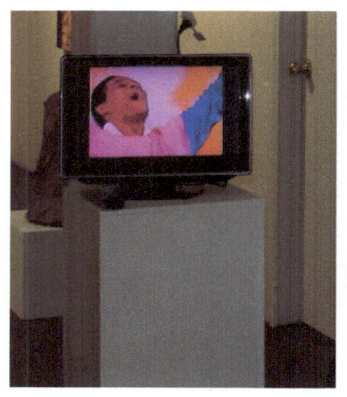
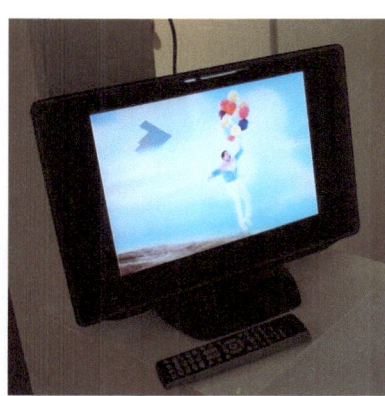
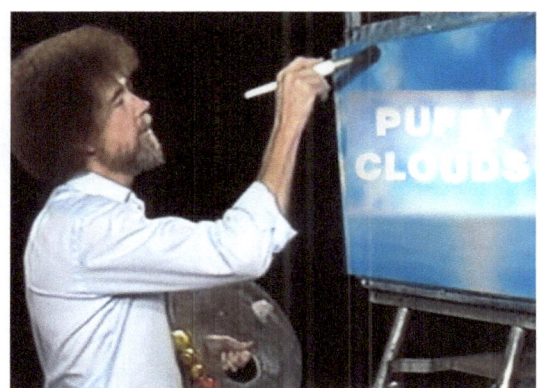

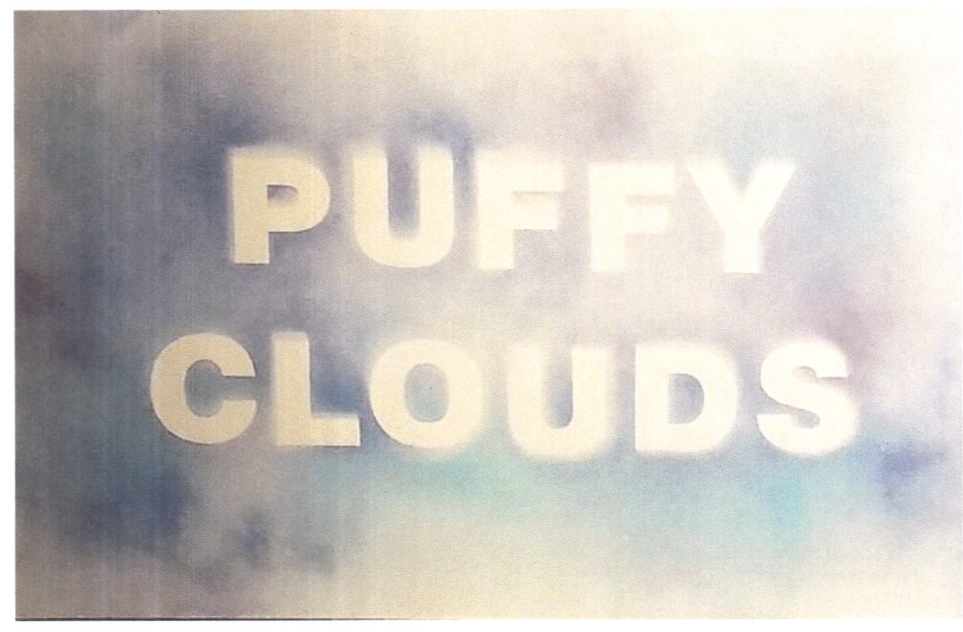

Title: "Puffy Clouds"
Medium: Aerosol on Canvas
Size: 18 x 24

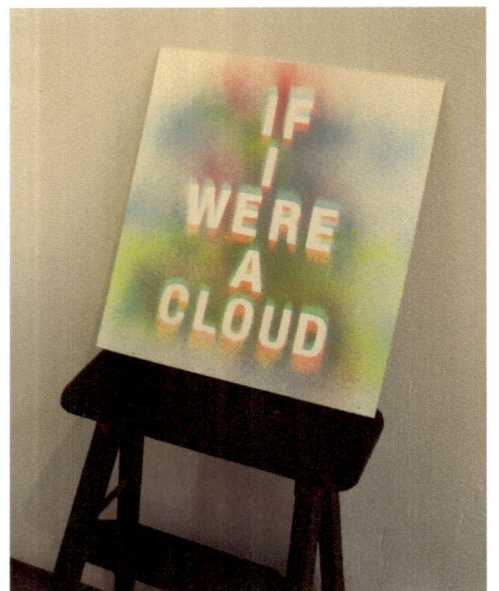

Title: "If I Were A Cloud"
Medium: Aerosol on Rag Board
Size: 9 x 12

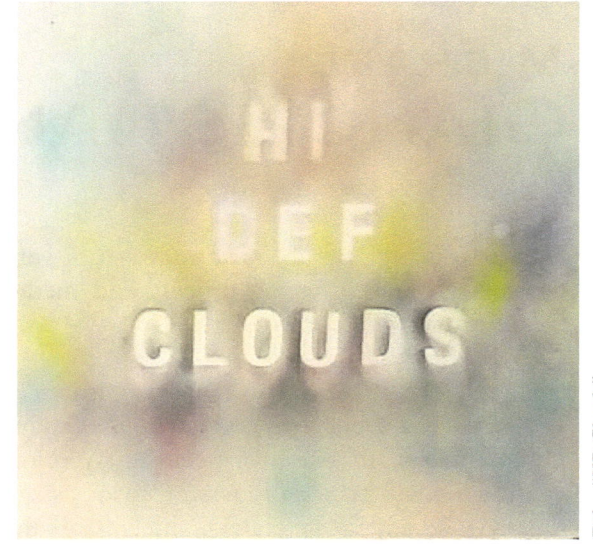

Title: "HD Clouds"
Medium: Aerosol on Canvas
Size: 16 x 16

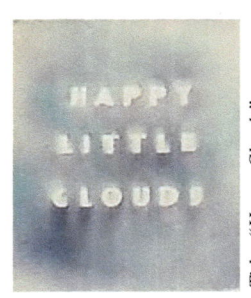
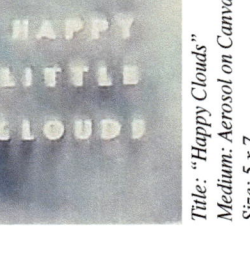

Title: "Happy Clouds"
Medium: Aerosol on Canvas
Size: 5 x 7

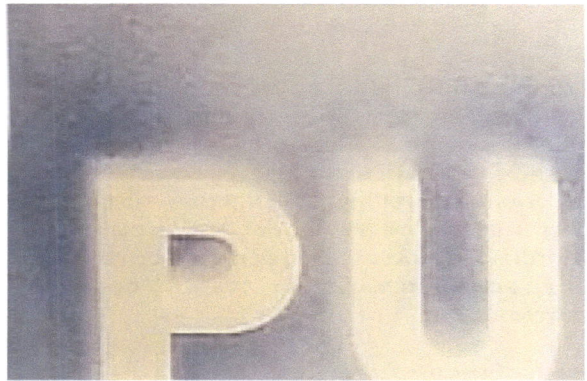
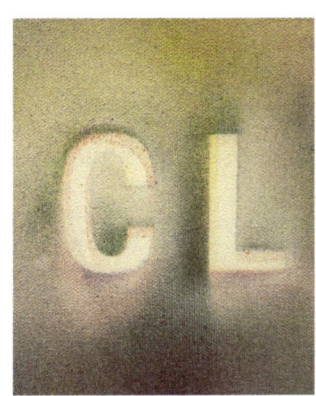
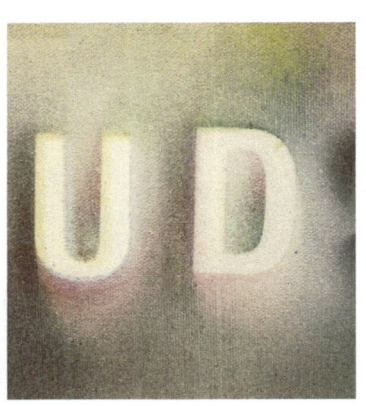

MICHAEL
GIANCRISTIANO

"Plywood is my primary medium to work with and I'm constantly reinventing my process and methods while creating new bodies of work."

Generally speaking, my work is geophysically abstract and earth related but recently I have been exploring a new moon concept. Rather than peel the layers of plywood apart, I use ball peen hammers of various size to pound the plywood and create craters. This mirrors the creation of the moon by asteroid collisions while speaking of man's primordial nature and evolution. The work is then painted and the sides are texture coated to resemble the surface of the moon.

What I've discovered is that it takes an enormous amount of energy to create one of these works and in doing so I was relieving all of my negative energy while simultaneously creating something very positive.

MICHAEL GIACRISTIANO WAS BORN IN LOS ANGELES CALIFORNIA AND IS AN ACCOMPLISHED ARTIST WITH OVER 25 YEARS OF EXHIBITION HISTORY. HE IS BEST KNOWN FOR HIS SCULPTED AND DECONSTRUCTED WOODEN WALL RELIEF THAT EXPLORE NATURE THROUGH THE MEDIUM OF PLYWOOD. MICHAEL HAS EXHIBITED INTERNATIONALLY AS WELL AS NATIONALLY AND CAN BE FOUND IN MANY PRIVATE AND CORPORATE COLLECTIONS.

HTTP://MICHAELGIANCRISTIANO.COM

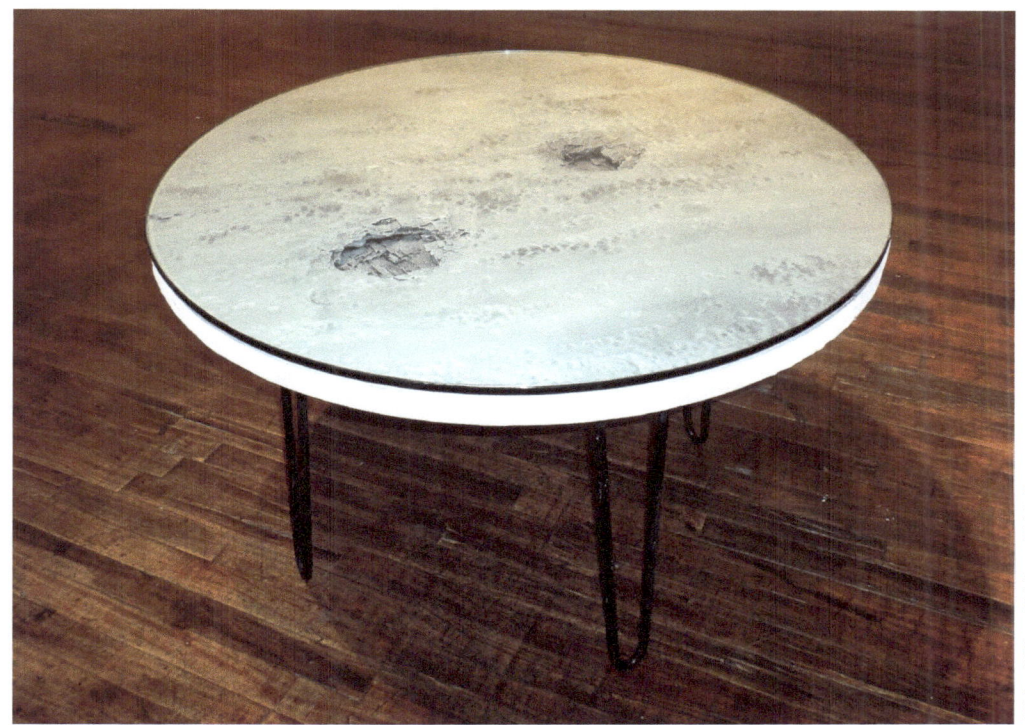

Title: "Thor-X Moon Table"
Medium: Mixed Media (plywood, acrylic, grout, glass, metal)
Dimensions: 36" diameter x 18"

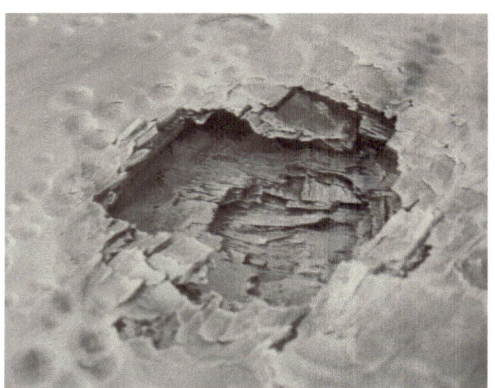
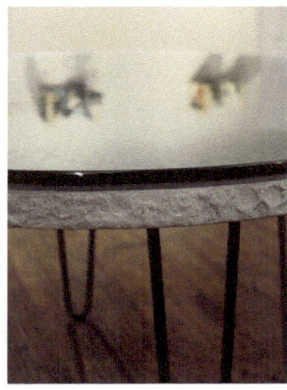
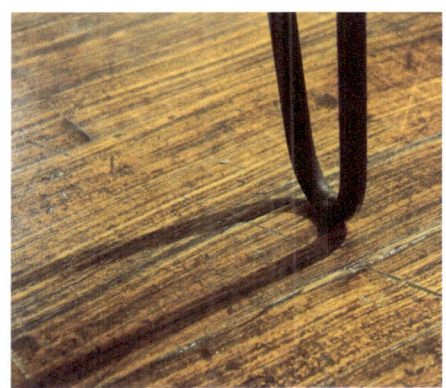

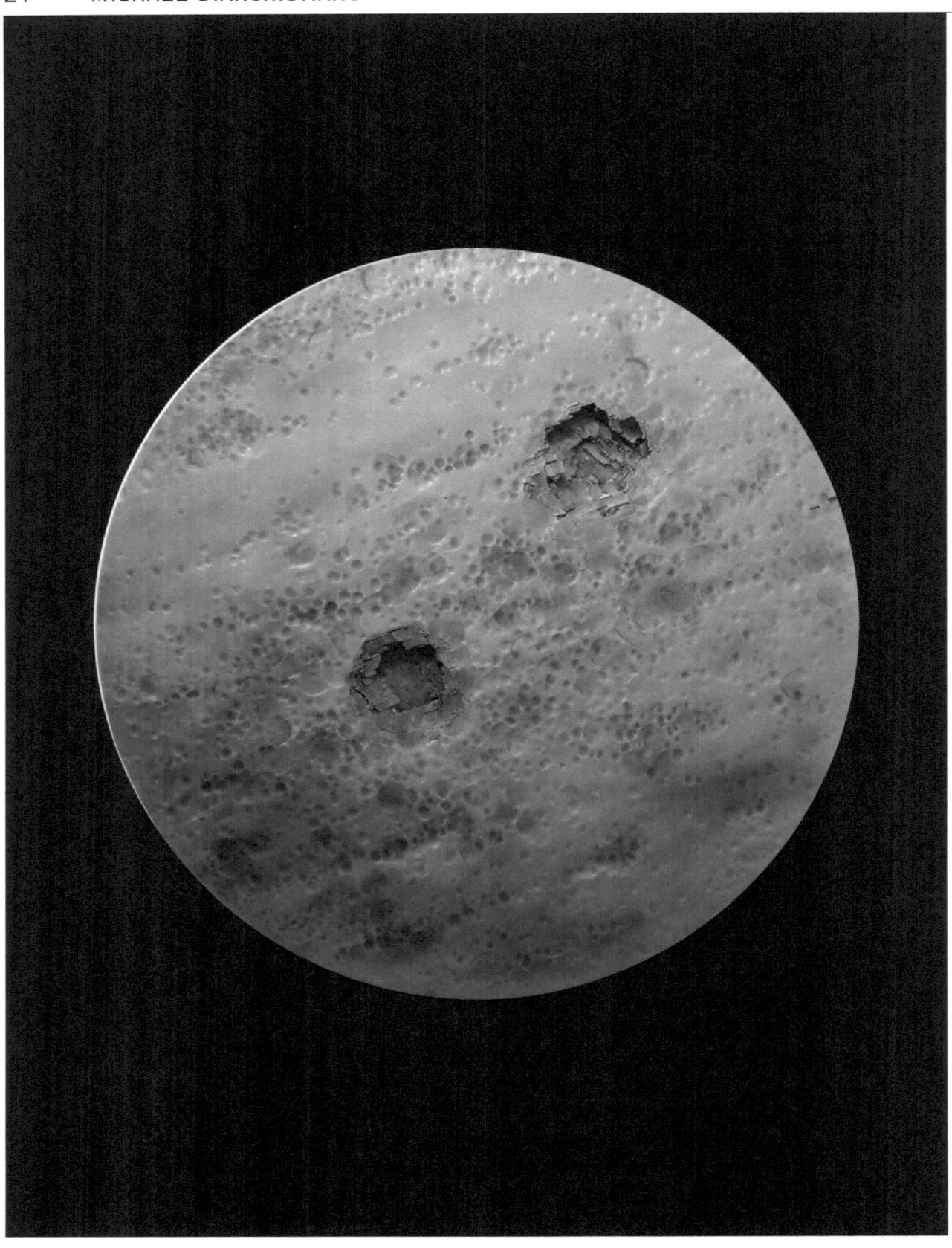

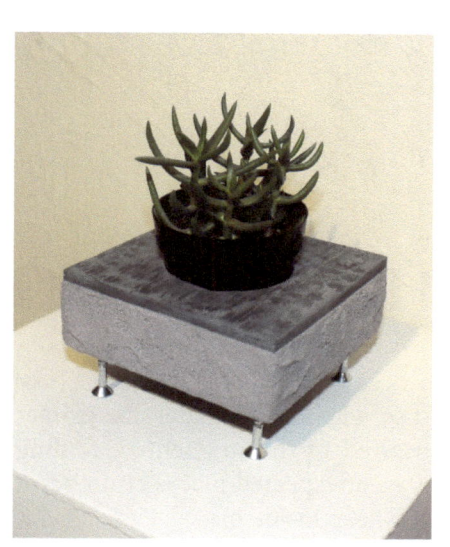

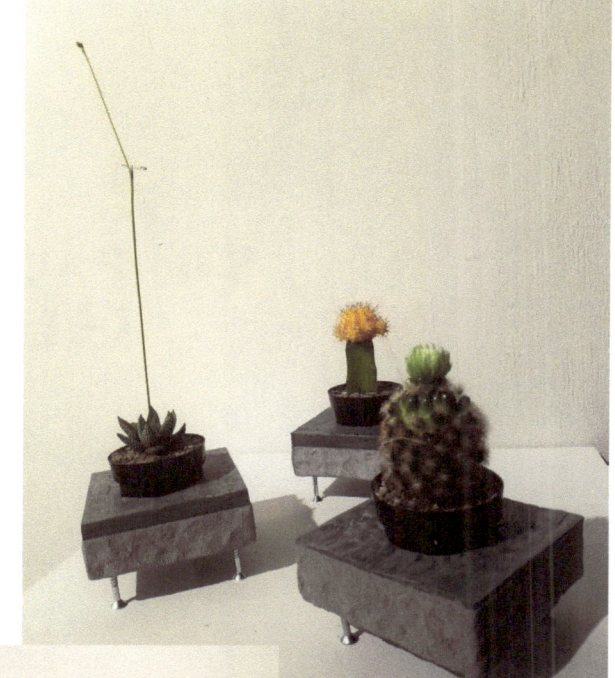

Title: "Moon Vessel" (#3, #6, #7, #8, #9, #10, #11, #12)
Medium: Mixed Media (plywood, acrylic, grout, glass, metal, plant)
Dimensions: 4" x 4" x 4"

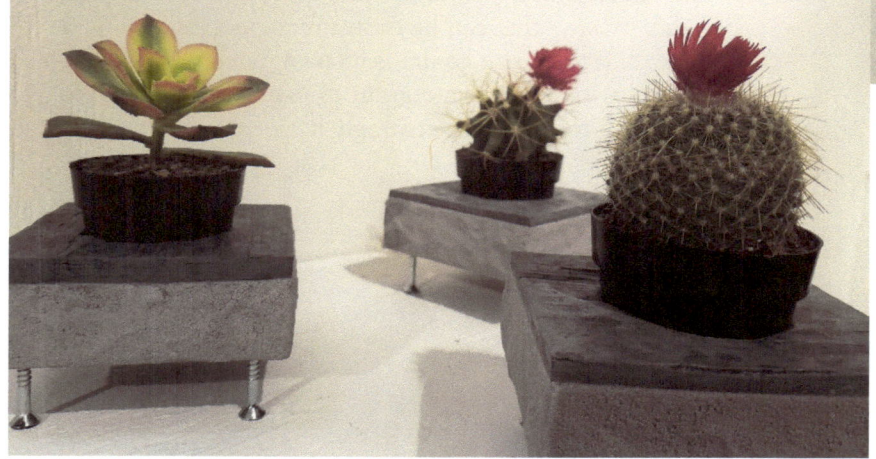

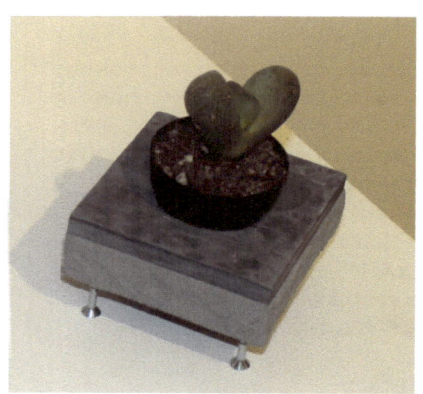

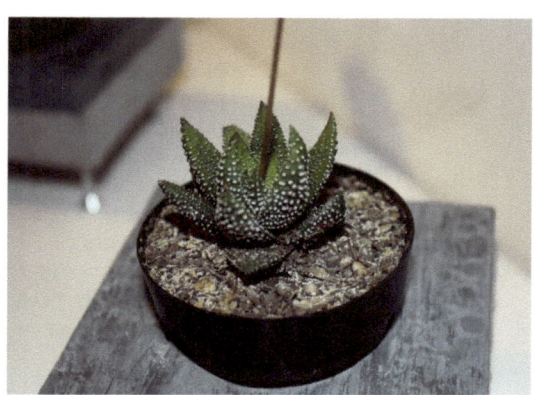

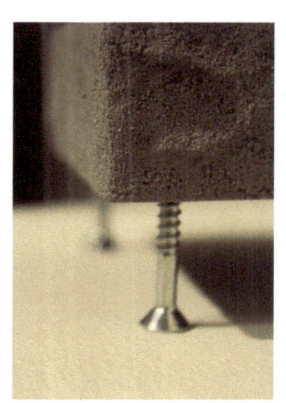

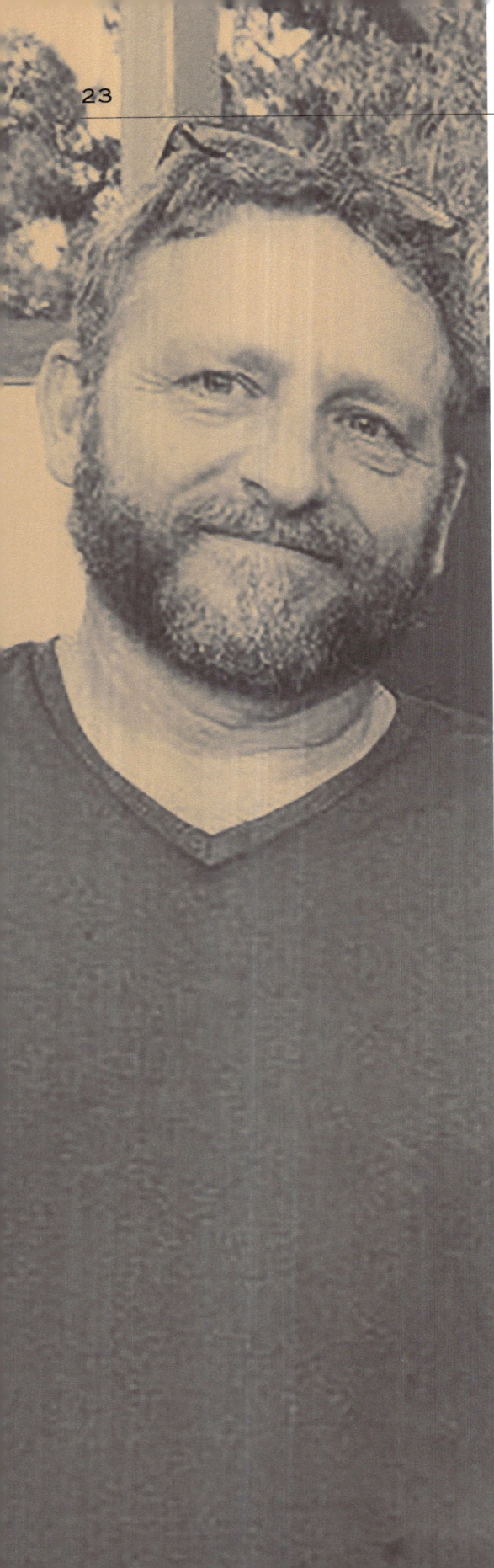

Paul
GUILLEMETTE

The art I make with found materials, primarily wood, is initially inspired in the moment of finding. Coming across beauty in unexpected places at no particular time stirs something deep inside me.

What I do with the materials back in my studio takes many different directions. Primarily, I seek to reveal that beauty in ways that can be funny, metaphorical, ironic or literal, and the result contains its own narrative: from living tree with an intricate grain of capillaries, to a cheap and useful material, to seemingly useless trash, to a thing of pure, deep beauty.

PAUL GUILLEMETTE'S WORK HAS BEEN EXHIBITED THROUGHOUT THE UNITED STATES IN BOTH SOLO AND GROUP EXHIBITIONS IN GALLERIES AND MUSEUMS. IMAGES OF HIS WORK HAVE BEEN PUBLISHED IN UC IRVINE'S JOURNAL OF ART AND LITERATURE AND IN THE UNIVERSITY OF MONTANA LITERARY MAGAZINE. HIS WORK IS IN THESE PERMANENT COLLECTIONS:
- MISSOULA MUSEUM OF ART, MISSOULA MT
- THE UNIVERSITY OF MONTANA, MISSOULA MT
- THE ARCHIE BRAY FOUNDATION FORTHE CERAMIC ARTS HELENA MT
- THE HOLTER MUSEUM OF ART, HELENA MT

HTTP://WWW.PAULGUILLEMETTE.COM

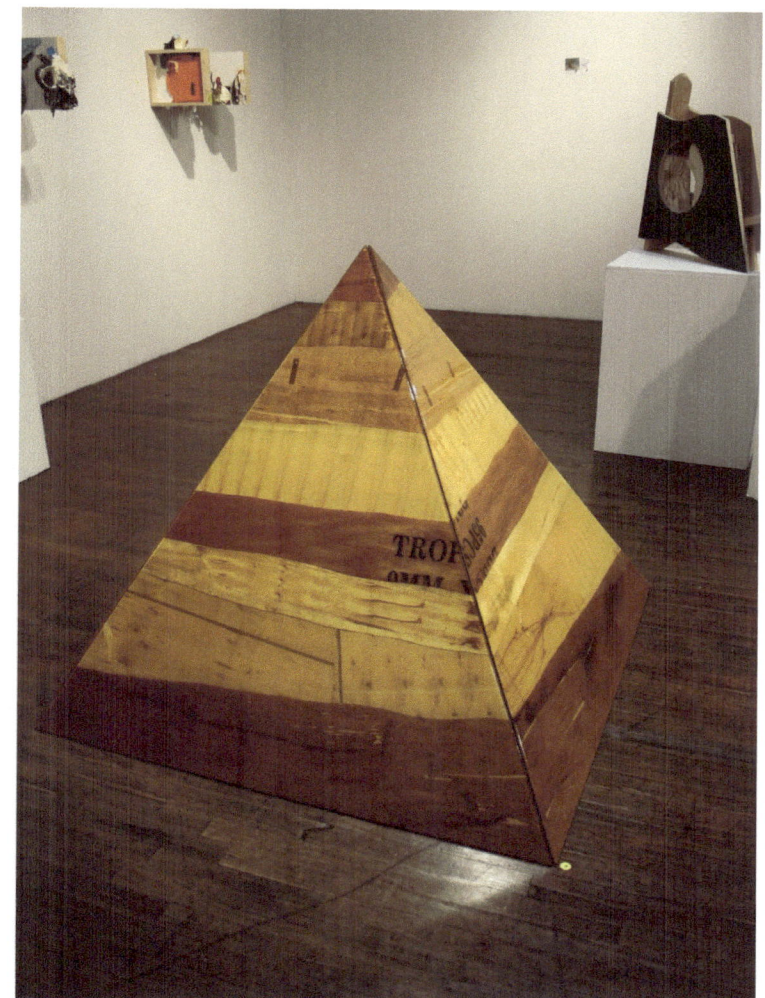

Title: "Pyramid #1"
Medium: Found Wood, Resin
Dimensions: 48" x 48" x 42"

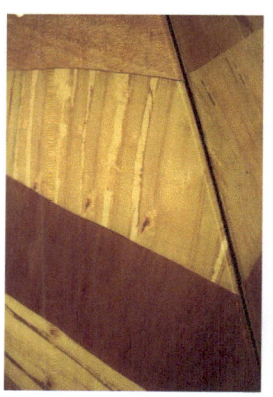
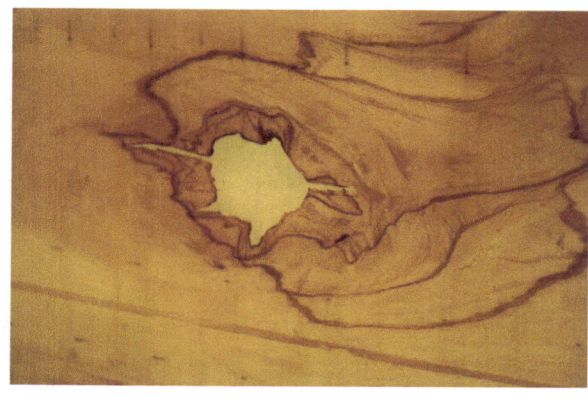
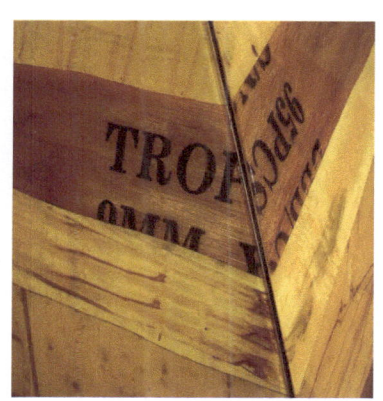

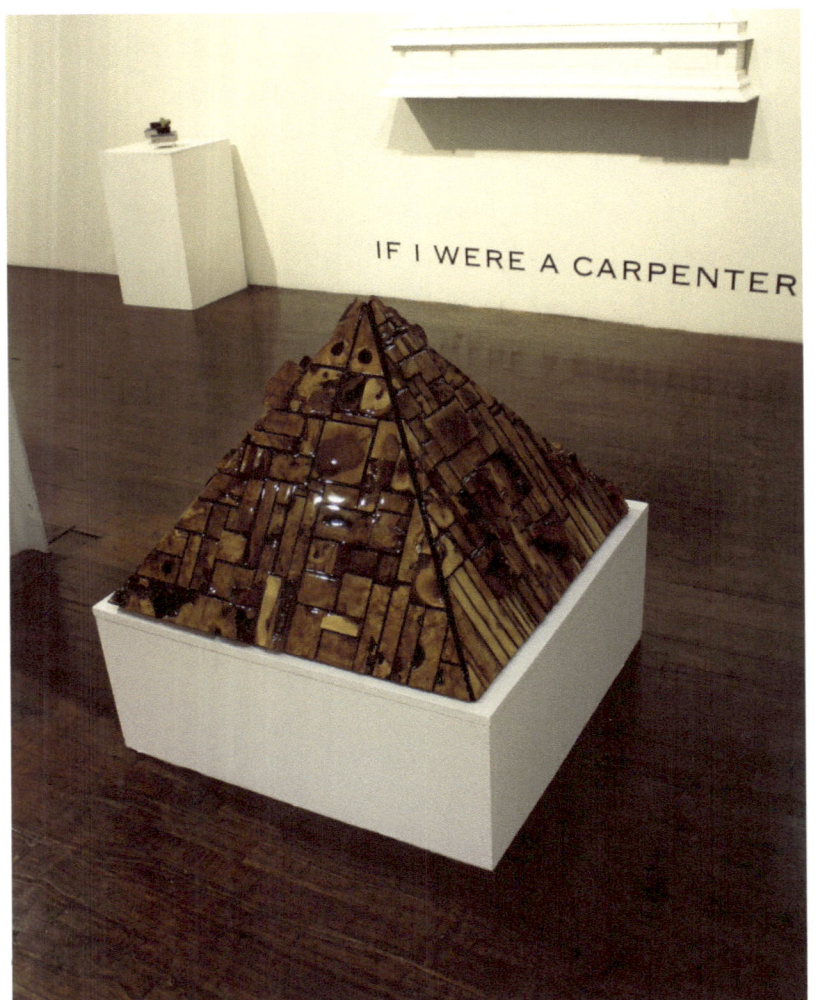

IF I WERE A CARPENTER

Title: "Pyramid #2"
Medium: Olive and Avocado Wood, Resin
Dimensions: 28" x 28" x 22"

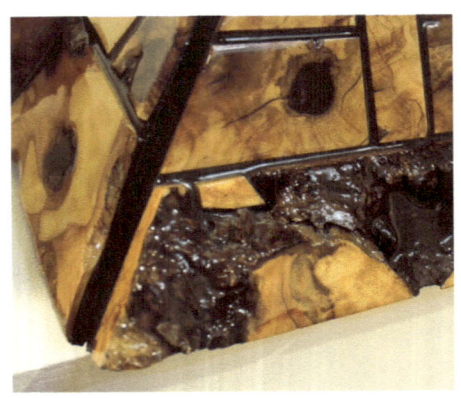

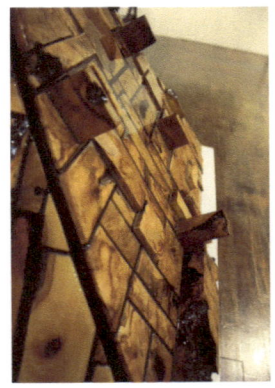

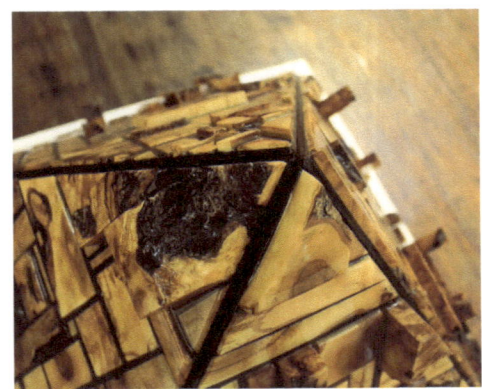

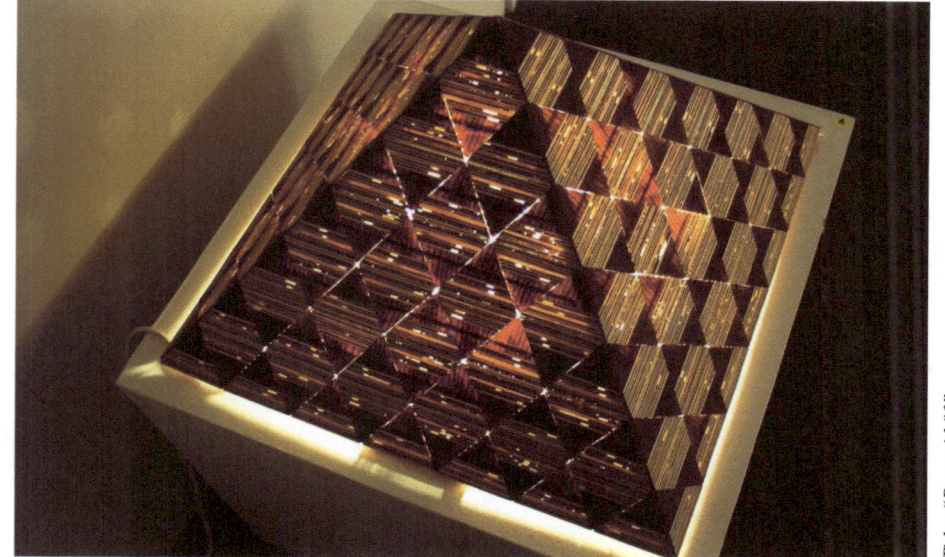

Title: "Pyramid # 3"
Medium: Plywood, Redwood, Resin, Electric Light
Dimensions: 21" x 21" x 14"

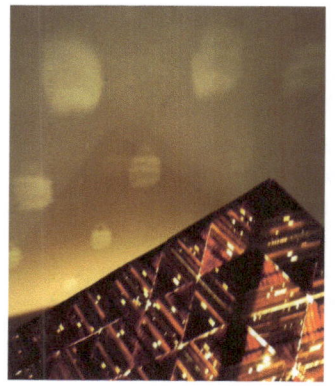
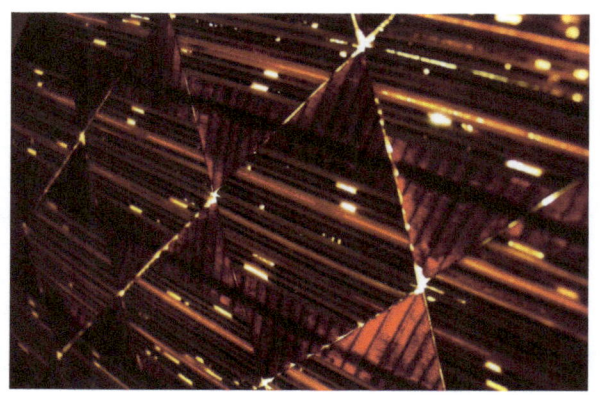
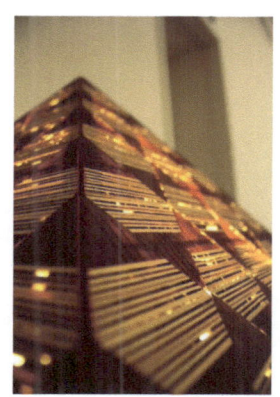

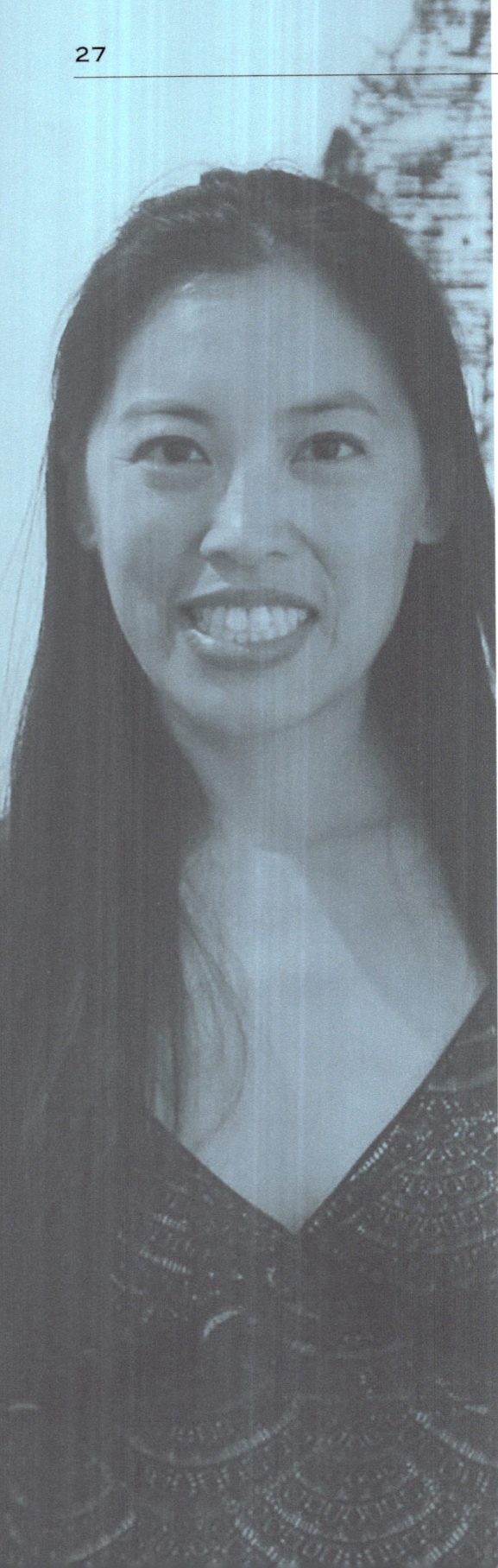

Flora
KAO

Flora Kao's installations examine the human impulse to order and preserve in the face of the uncontrollable. House Scroll explores the poignant associations of a collapsed desert homestead through life-size rubbings of its debris field. Executed on thirteen scrolls of paper, each thirty feet long, gestural black marks map the cabin at a specific moment of decay. Mapping absence and presence, the scrolls are unfurled vertically across the gallery wall. Capturing the physical evidence of failure, the rubbings archive the effect of entropy on a humble and beloved architecture form. House Scroll offers a visceral encounter with erasure and accumulation, meditating on the fugitive nature of home and the ease of loss in a land of new beginnings. House Scroll is the most recent manifestation of Kao's Homestead project which documents a trio of Wonder Valley's abandoned desert homesteads through installation, rubbings, photography, and writing.

KAO'S WORK EXPLORES THE POETICS OF HUMAN RELATIONSHIP WITH ENVIRONMENT. EXAMINING ARCHITECTURE AND TECHNOLOGY, KAO TRANSFORMS EVERYDAY STRUCTURES INTO SYSTEMS OF BEAUTY. KAO HAS EXHIBITED EXTENSIVELY SUCH AS AT THE PASADENA MUSEUM OF CALIFORNIA ART AND THE MUSEUM OF CONTEMPORARY ART IN BEIJING.

HTTP://FLORATKAO.BLOGSPOT.COM

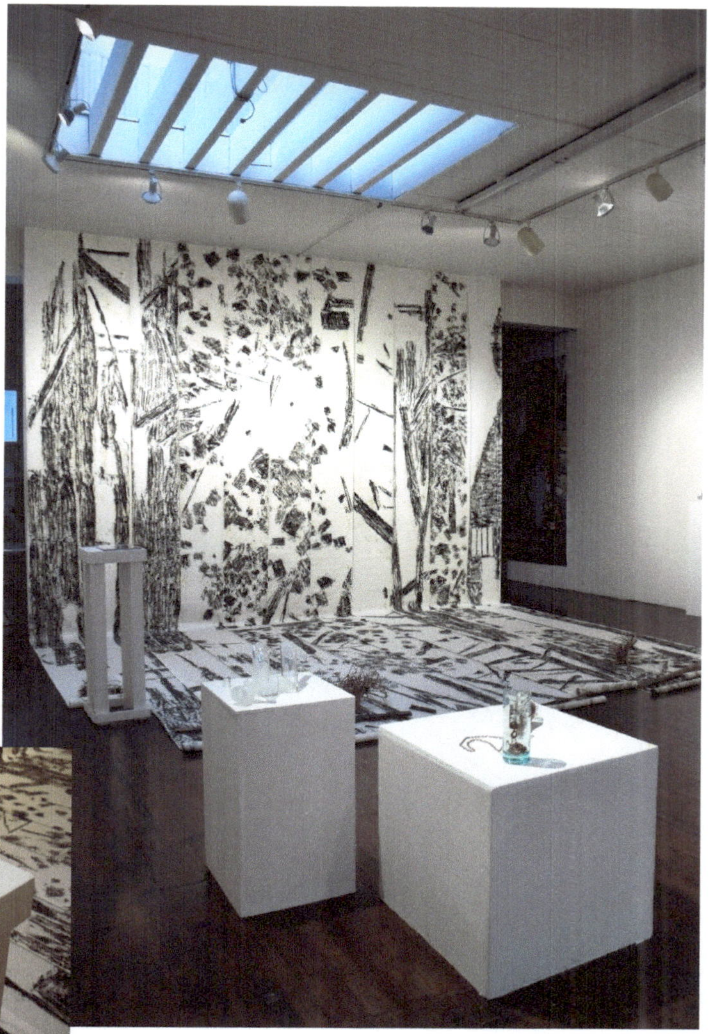

Title: "House Scroll"
Medium: Oil Stick Rubbing on Rice Paper, Remnants from Desert Homestead
Dimensions: 11 scrolls; 18"x30" each

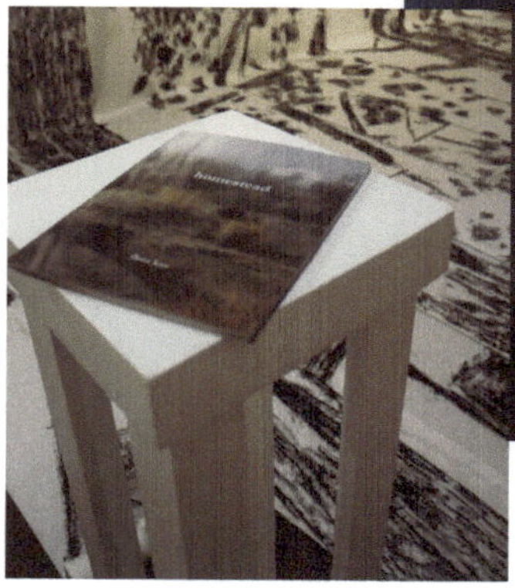

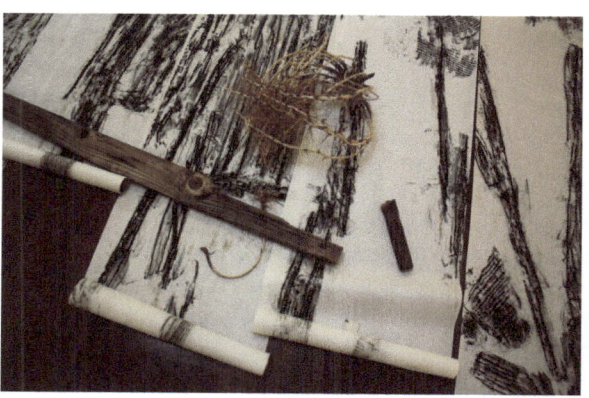
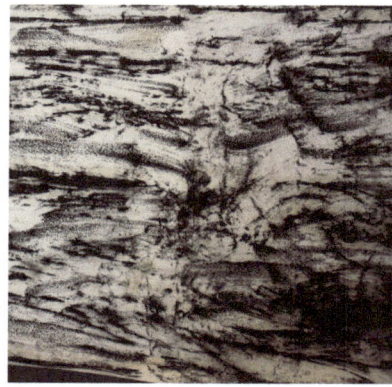
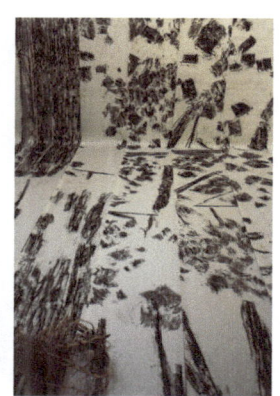

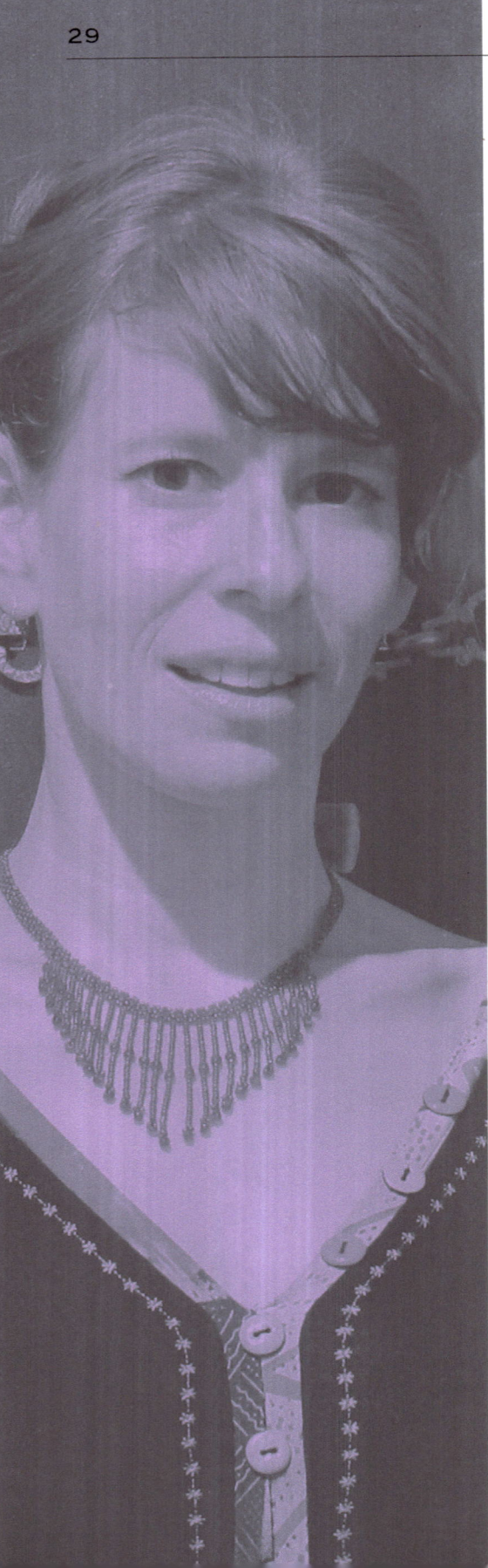

Rachel Lauren
KASTER

I am a sculptor:

My primary mediums are glass, wood and steel.
I create, I consume, I destroy, I observe, I internalize, and I respond.
I am told facts that I must never forget to question.
I am told there are rules but I refuse to be confined.
I am limited only by the laws of physics.
I am a part of everything of this earth.
I affirm my existence through the tradition of manipulation and transformation.
I begin my process with personal conversations and I realize my thoughts through form, material and color.
I utilize structure to draw upon association.
I strive to create sculptural objects that are compelling.
I engage the viewer with familiar objects and beckon the observer to create their own narrative.

RACHEL LAUREN KASTER IS A MULTI-MEDIA ARTIST, PERFORMER AND EDUCATOR WHOSE WORK HAS BEEN EXHIBITED THROUGHOUT THE UNITED STATES. SHE EARNED HER BFA AT THE MASSACHUSETTS COLLEGE OF ART, HOLDS AN MFA FROM THE ROCHESTER INSTITUTE OF TECHNOLOGY AND CURRENTLY LIVES AND CREATES IN LOS ANGELES.

HTTP://WWW.RACHELKASTER.COM

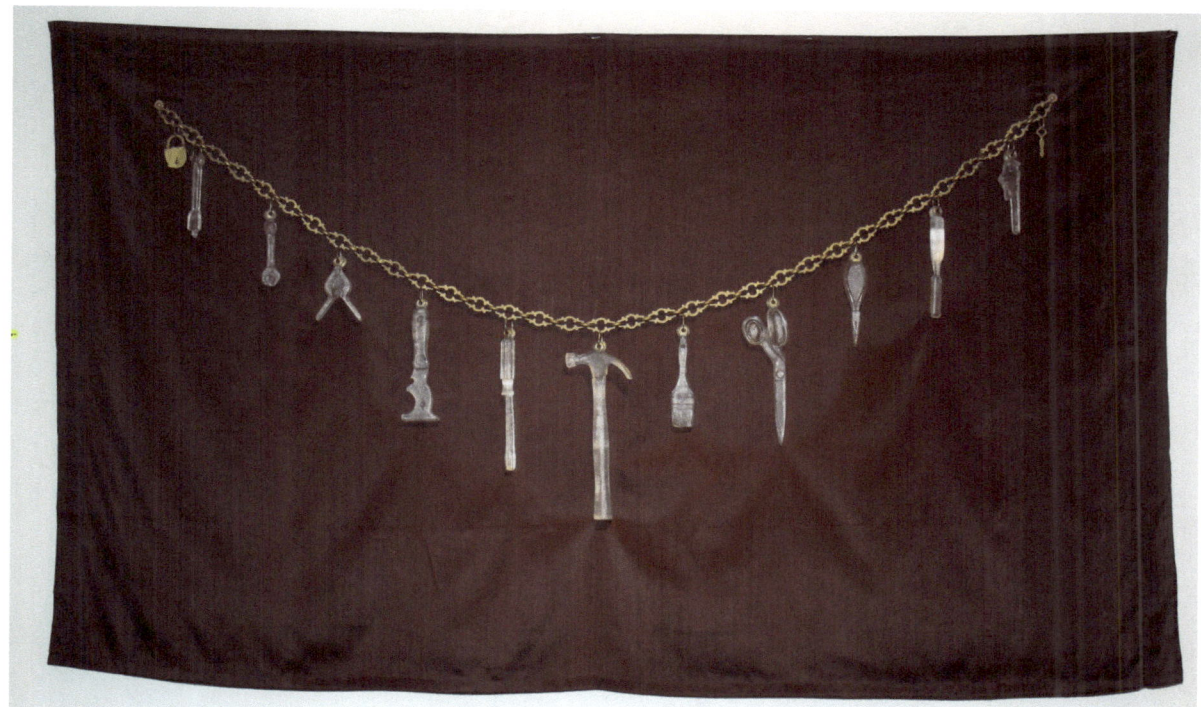

Title: "Lessons Learned"
Medium: Brass, Glass, Found Object
Dimensions: 67" x 26"

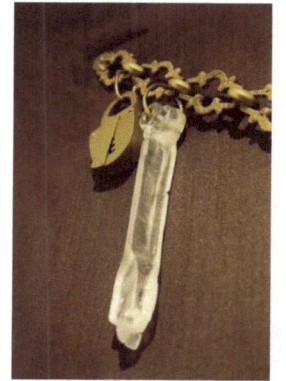 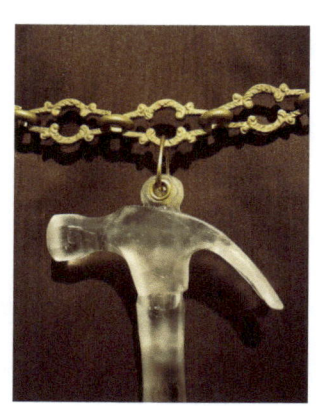 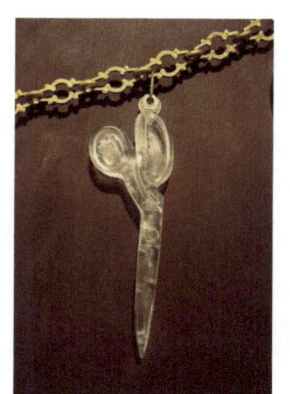 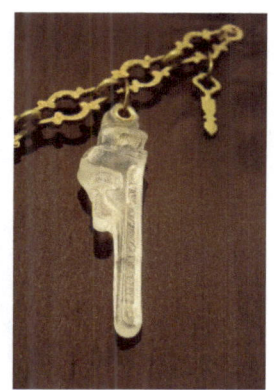

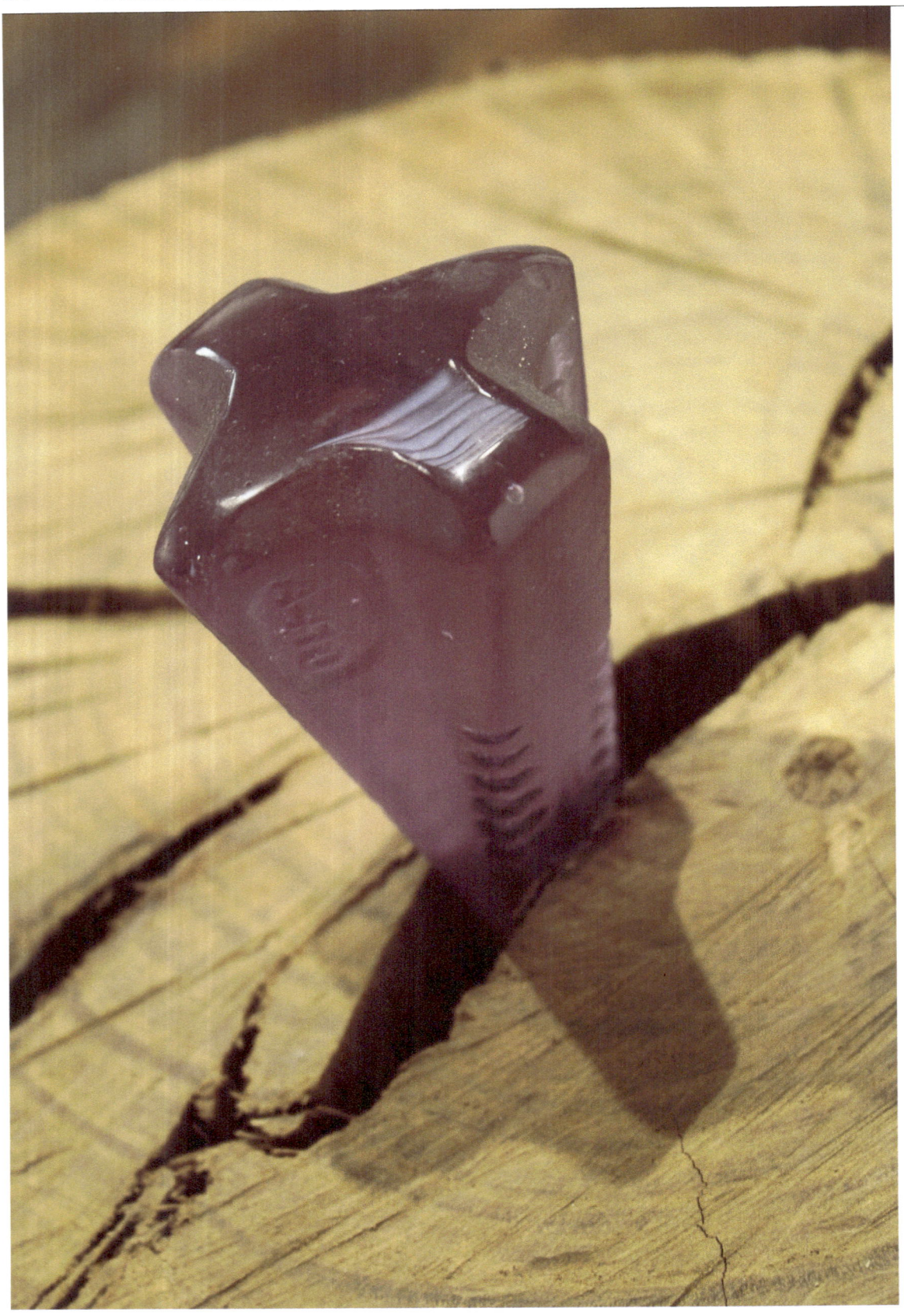

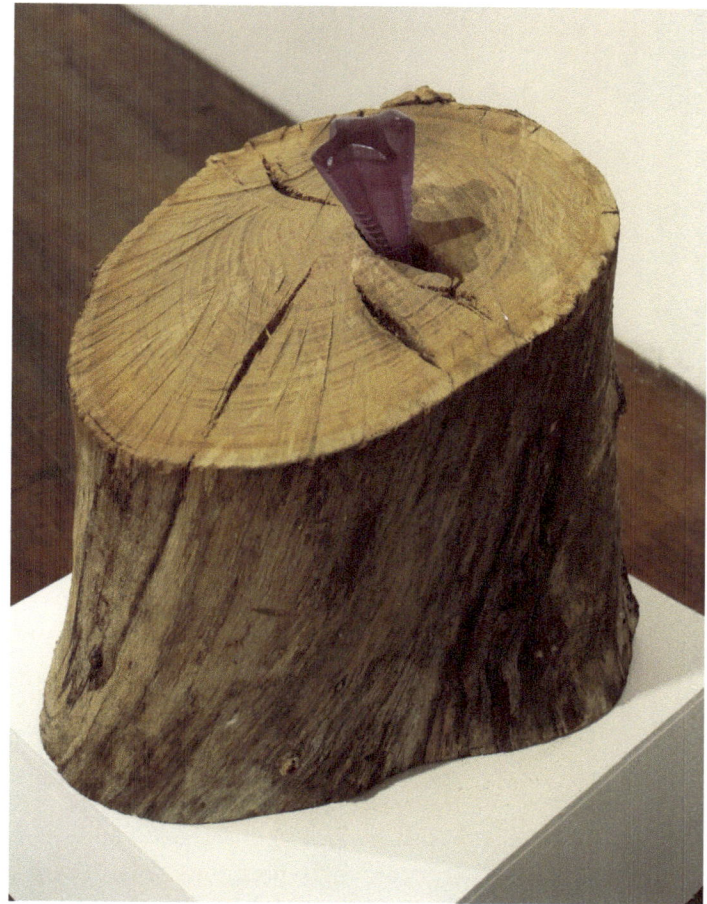

Title: "Shall We Stay Together"
Medium: Tree Stump, Glass
Dimensions: 16" x 16" x 26"

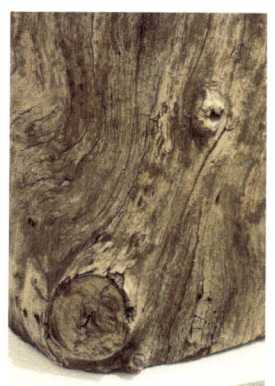 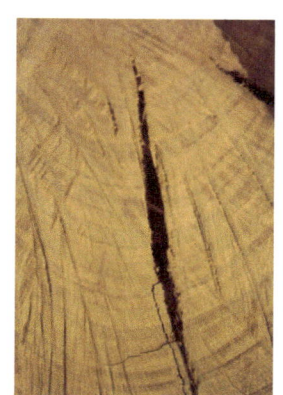 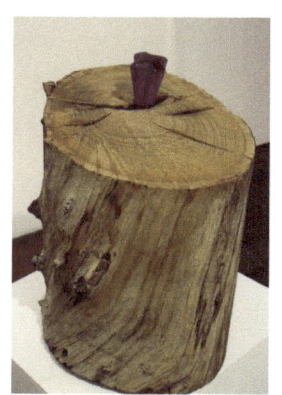 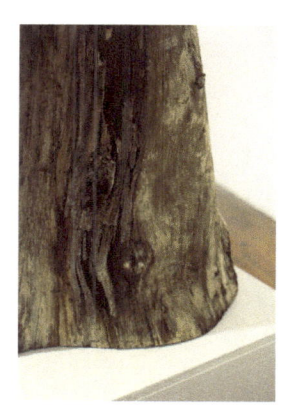

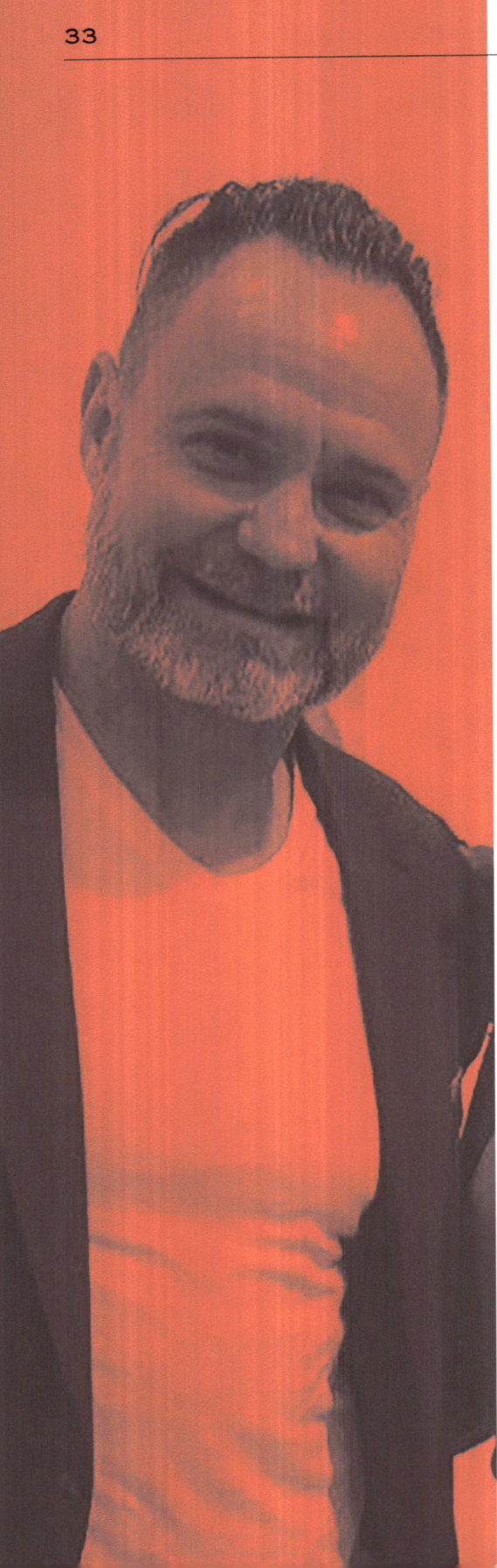

Chris
MERCIER

My work explores and attempts to redefine the workings of the Pictorial Window and its relationship to two and three dimensional space. It does this by repositioning (reframing?) the act of framing (the paintings edges) and altering both the location and condition of separation created by the picture plane.

The works consist of a construction of multi-connected panels, set in a various three dimensional orientations that collect, enclose and start to define a condition of actual physical space. Within these new physically defined spaces, on, across and between the panels I reinsert the 'act of painting'. A repositioning starts to occur with numerous picture planes in various physical orientations appear. The viewer no longer has a single place to view or stand to try to comprehend the work. There are now spatial cavities, canyons and pockets to explore. These new unfolded and semi concealed spaces become opportunities to find and reinvent 'Painting'. They not only challenge its place but they also start to question its formal characteristics. Within this potential new paradigm the 'act of painting' now finds itself in a dual position, one of traditional image making but one also of physical space/form making.

MERCIER IS AN ARTIST AND ARCHITECT PRACTICING IN INGLEWOOD, CALIFORNIA WHERE HE OPENED HIS ARCHITECTURAL PRACTICE. EARNING HIS BACHELOR OF SCIENCE DEGREE IN ARCHITECTURE AT LAWRENCE UNIVERSITY, HE LATER RECEIVED HIS MASTERS IN ARCHITECTURE FROM THE SOUTHERN CALIFORNIA INSTITUTE OF ARCHITECTURE.

HTTP://WWW.FERSTUDIO.COM

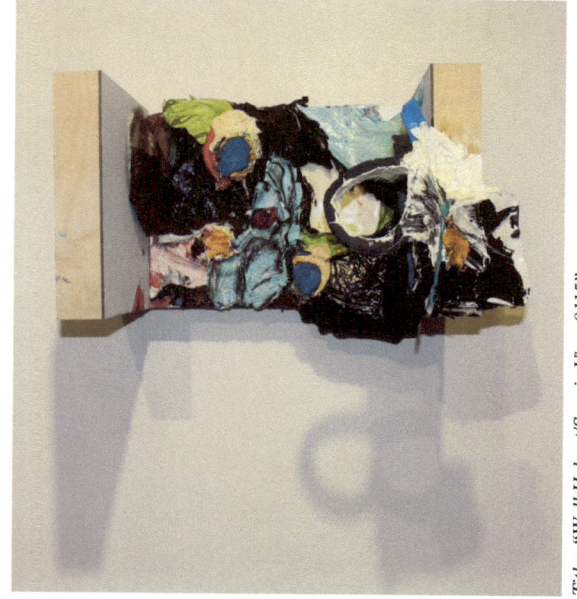

Title: "Wall Helmet/Scenic View-0115"
Medium: Oil, Ink, Latex, and Enamel on Wood Panel Construction
Dimensions: 11"x 18.5" x 14"

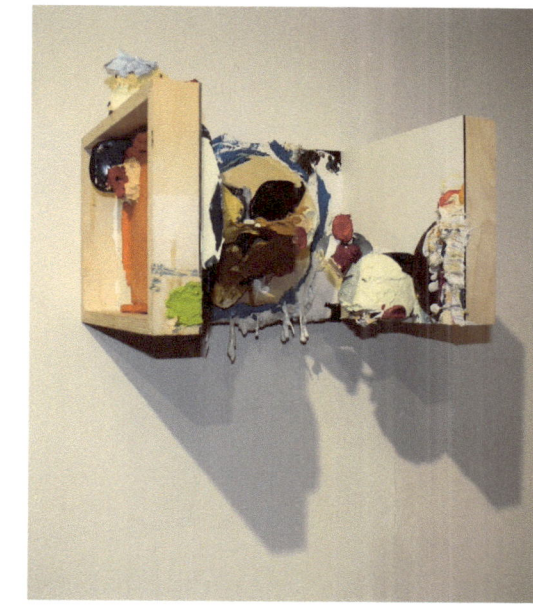

Title: "Wall Helmet/Scenic View-0215-016"
Medium: Oil, Ink, Latex, and Enamel on Wood Panel Construction
Dimensions: 11"x 18.5" x 14"

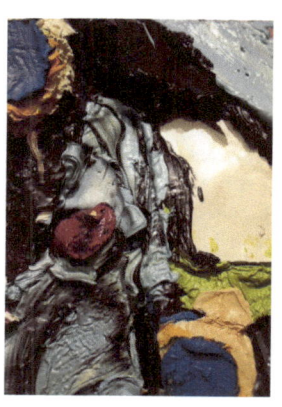
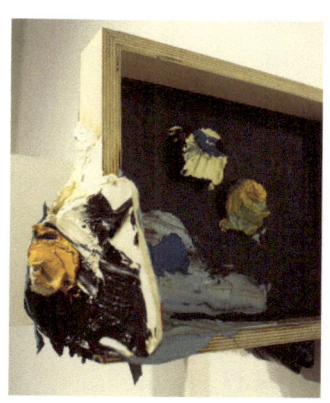
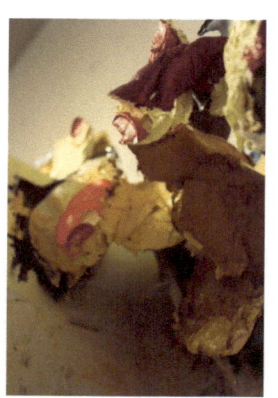
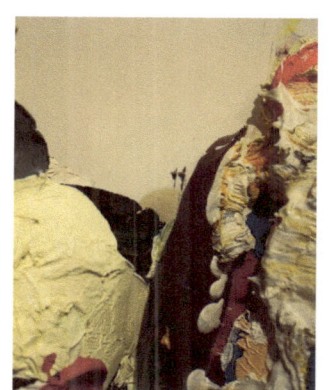

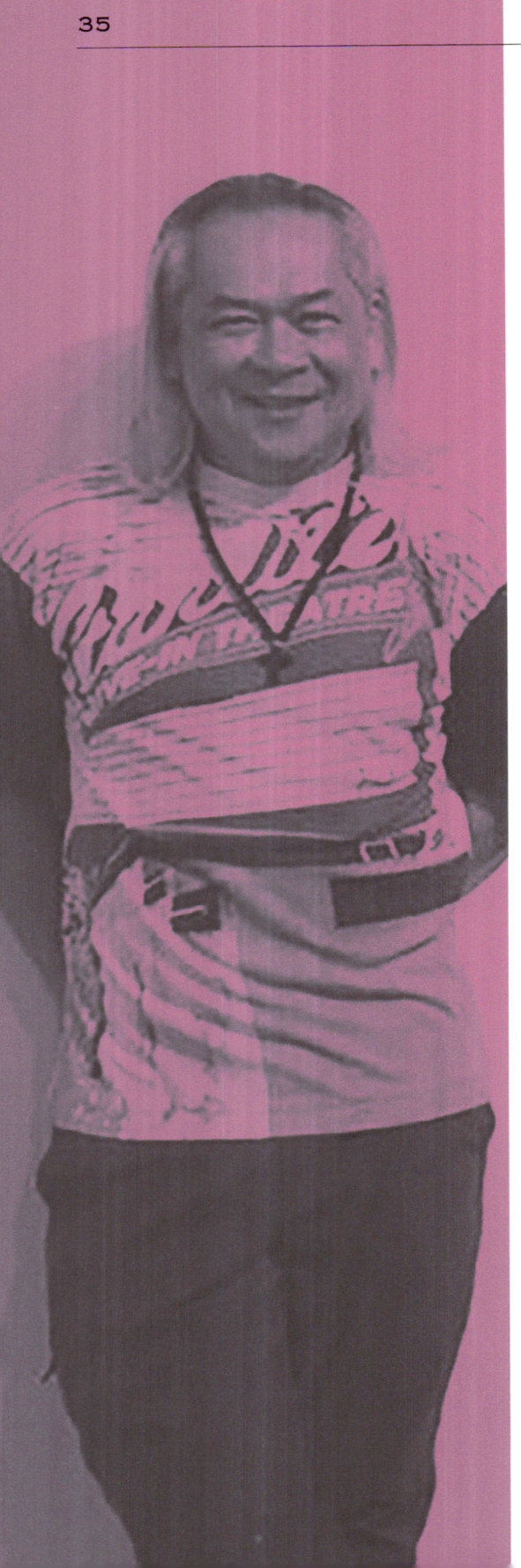

HUNG VIET
NGUYEN

"If I were a carpenter, then I would carve out - remove the excess! But I was building up - putting on the medium. It does not matter as long as I get the same result."

-Hung

HUNG VIET NGUYEN WAS BORN IN VIETNAM WHERE HE STUDIED BIOLOGY AT SCIENCE UNIVERSITY IN SAIGON, VIETNAM, THEN TRANSITIONED TO WORKING AS AN ILLUSTRATOR, GRAPHIC ARTIST AND DESIGNER SINCE SETTLEMENT IN THE U.S. IN 1982. HONORS INCLUDE THE JUROR'S CHOICE AWARDS, 2013, AND THE SAN DIEGO ART INSTITUTE BIENNIAL INTERNATIONAL AWARD EXHIBITION, 2015.

HTTP://HUNG4ART.COM

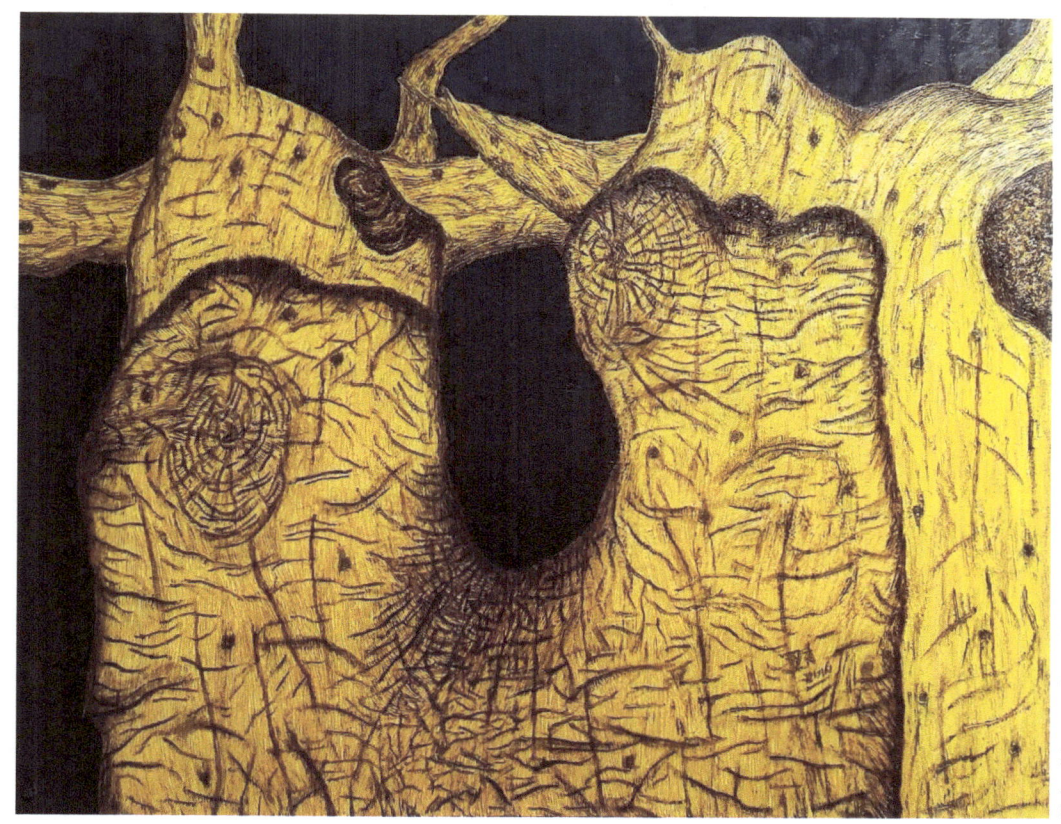

Title: "Ancient Pine #20"
Medium: Oil on Canvas
Dimensions: 48" x 60"

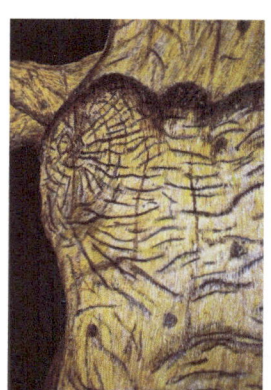 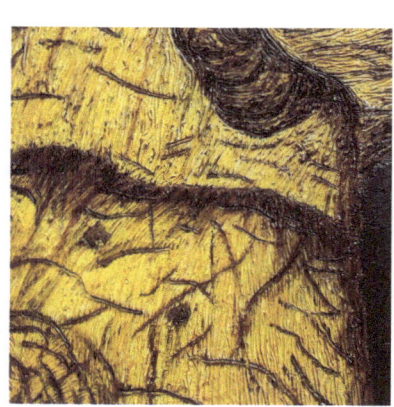 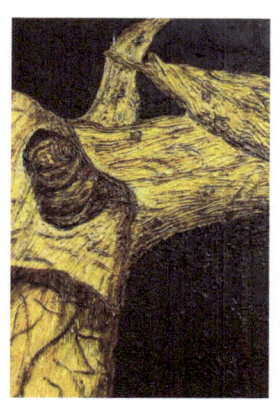 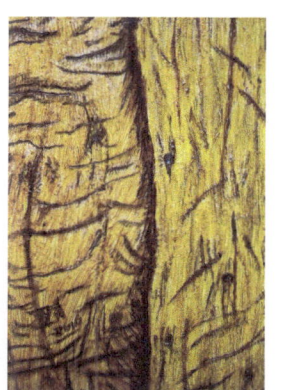

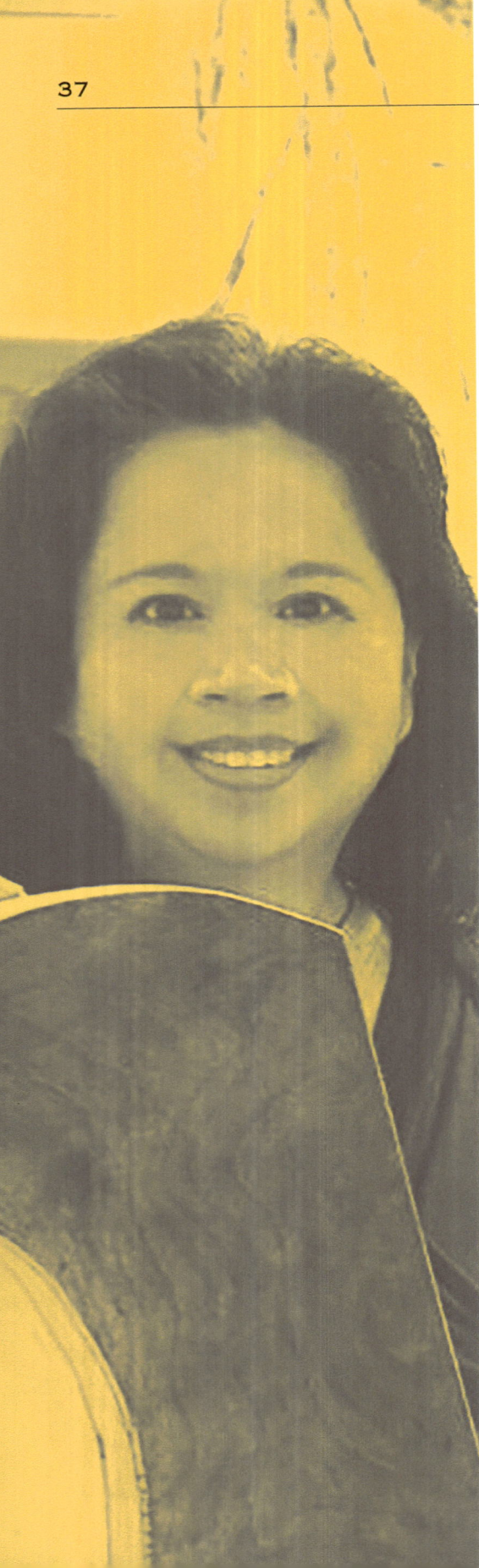

ELLEN
RIINGEN

The practice of mapping multiple conditions of our built environment has always been both challenging and elusive. Inspired by the Japanese haikus that have the ability to convey complex human experiences in concise poetry, my artwork emphasizes the importance of creating balance from the marks we make in society for future generations to thrive. These "visual haikus," as I am calling them are meant to bring the onlooker's subjective experiences to the poetic physical and emotional spirit of a place made up of layers of histories, cultures, beliefs, and hopes. Each piece strives to transform rich complexities into modern simplicity, transcending realities to progress the evolution of the human spirit or consciousness.

The layering and carving techniques of mixed media on wood has allowed me to transform these multiplicities to create each "visual haiku," attempting to map the spiritual as well as the physical. Using wood allows me to bring in tactile sensibilities that make up built forms while bringing out its beauty from its original being, the tree. Both techniques allow me to explore blurring the two-dimensional and three-dimensional realms in very different ways.

The "visual haiku" is my meditation to go beyond the visible to the spiritual resonance that exists, allowing us to confront ourselves; striving to see the differences and revealing its beauty.

ELLEN RIINGEN IS A SOUTHERN CALIFORNIA VISUAL ARTIST, ARCHITECTURAL DESIGNER, AND INTEGRATIVE HEALER. SHE RECEIVED A MASTERS OF ARCHITECTURE DEGREE FROM THE AVANT-GARDE SCHOOL OF SOUTHERN CALIFORNIA INSTITUTE OF ARCHITECTURE. HER MIXED-MEDIA WORKS REVEAL AN APPRECIATION TO NATURE AND OUR RELATIONSHIP WITHIN IT.

HTTP://ELLENRIINGEN.COM

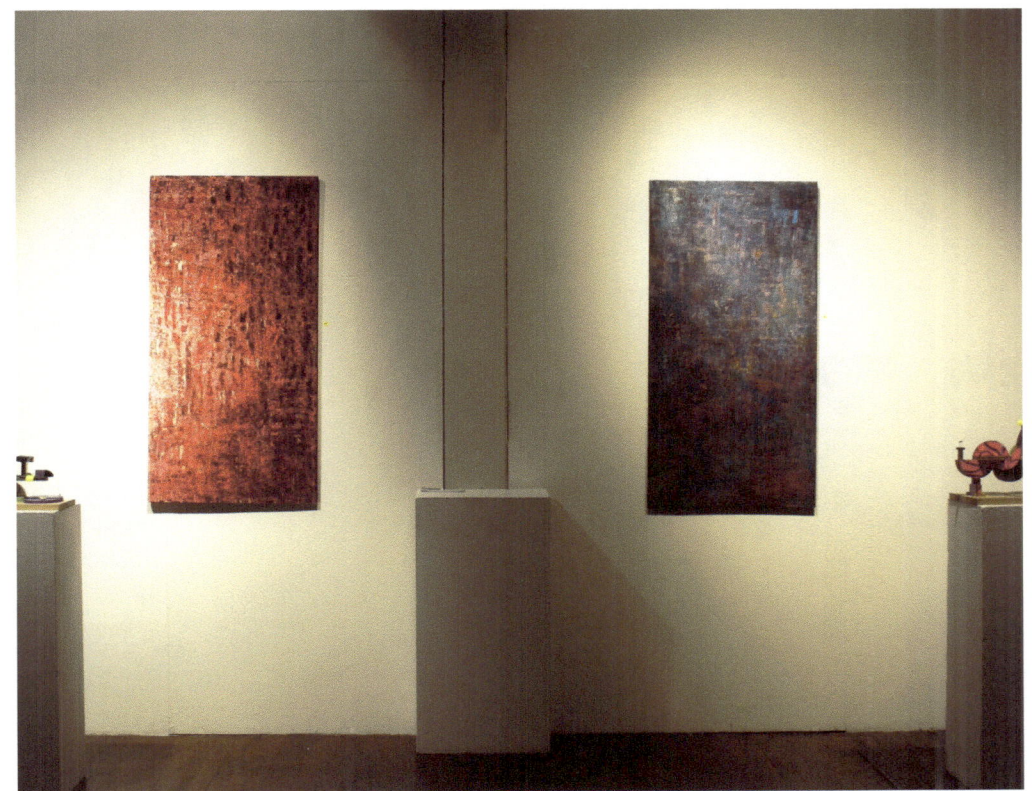

Title: "Urban Innocence" (left) and "Camiguin" (right)
Medium: Mixed Media
Dimensions: 24" x 48" each

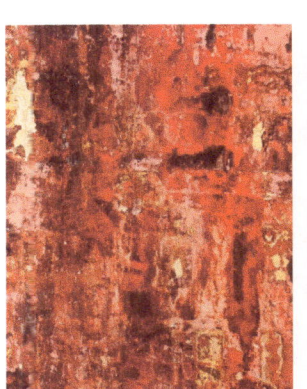
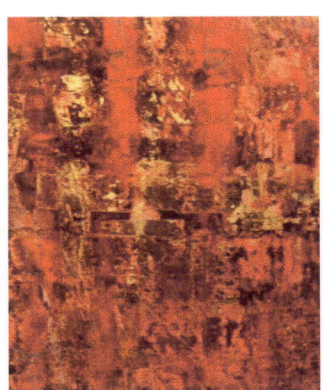
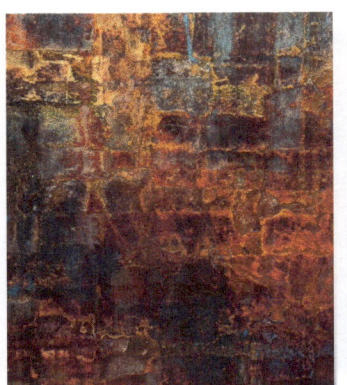
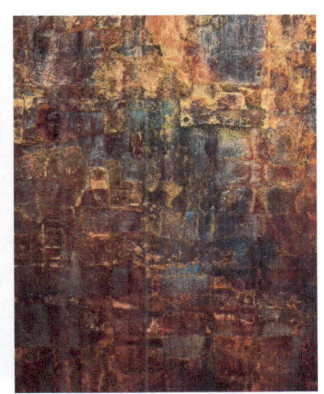

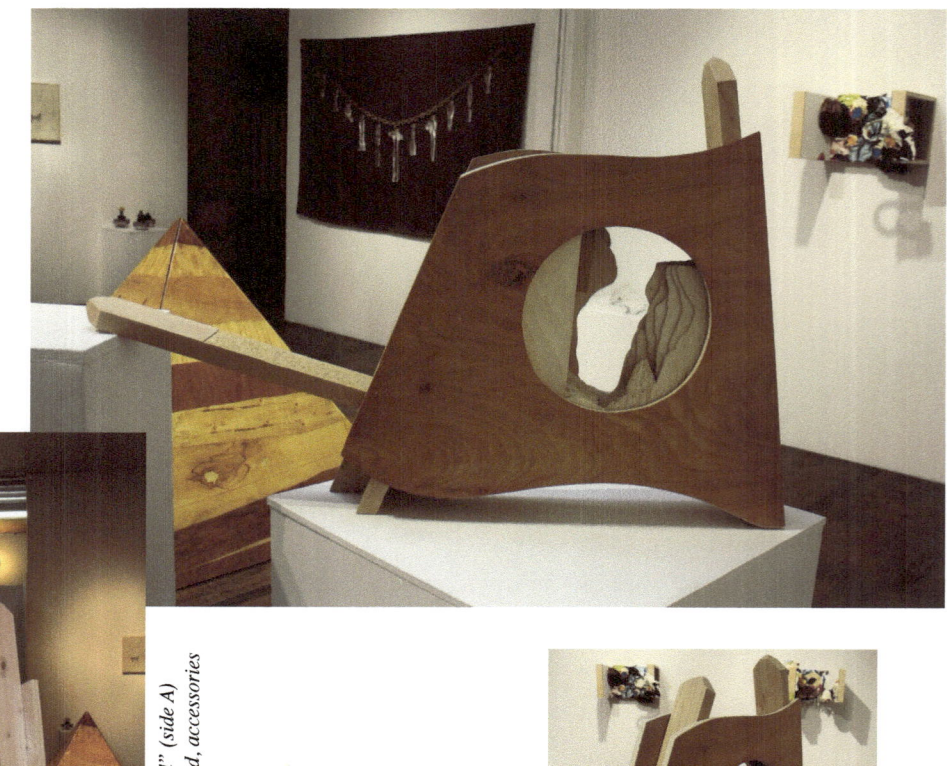

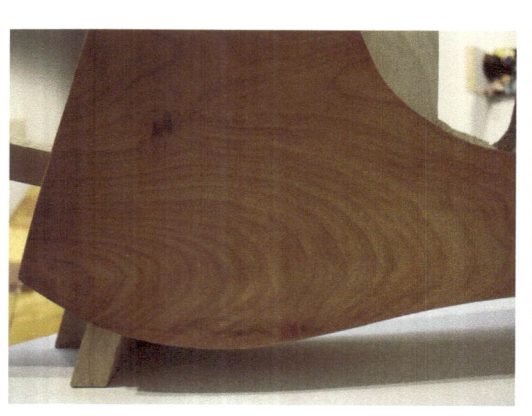

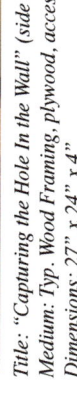

Title: "Capturing the Hole In the Wall" (side A)
Medium: Typ. Wood Framing, plywood, accessories
Dimensions: 27" x 24" x 4"

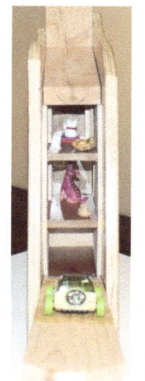

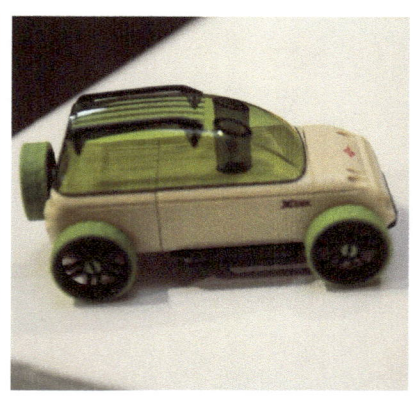

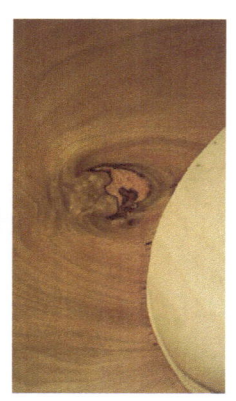

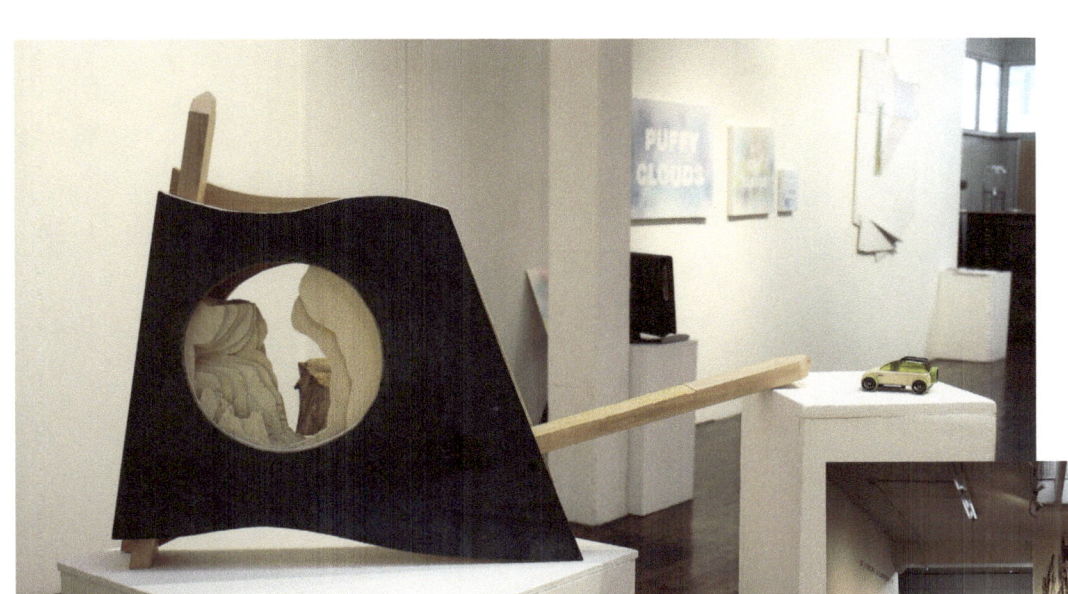

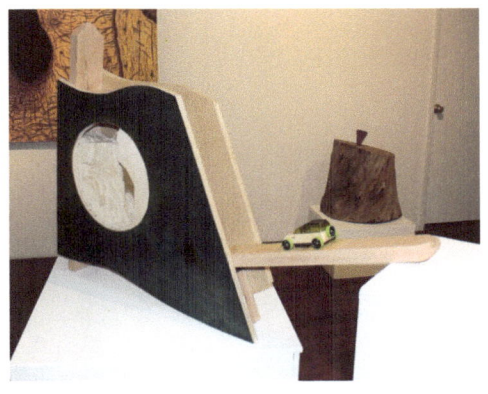

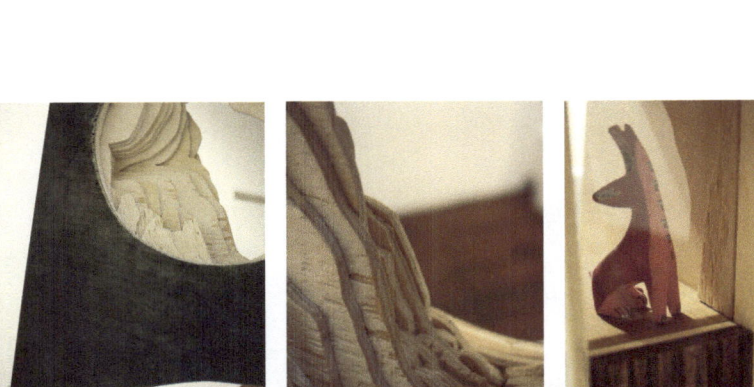

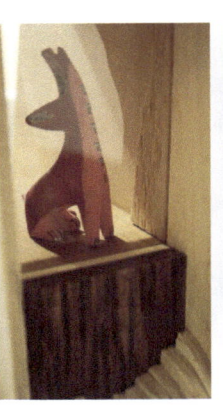

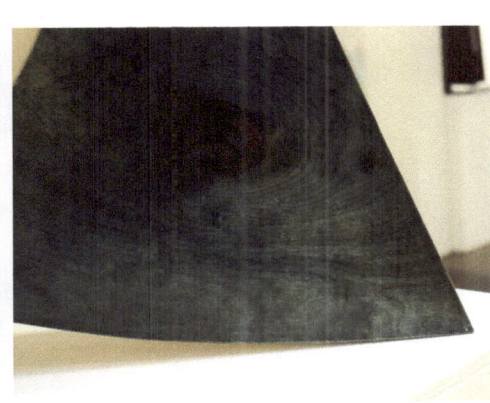

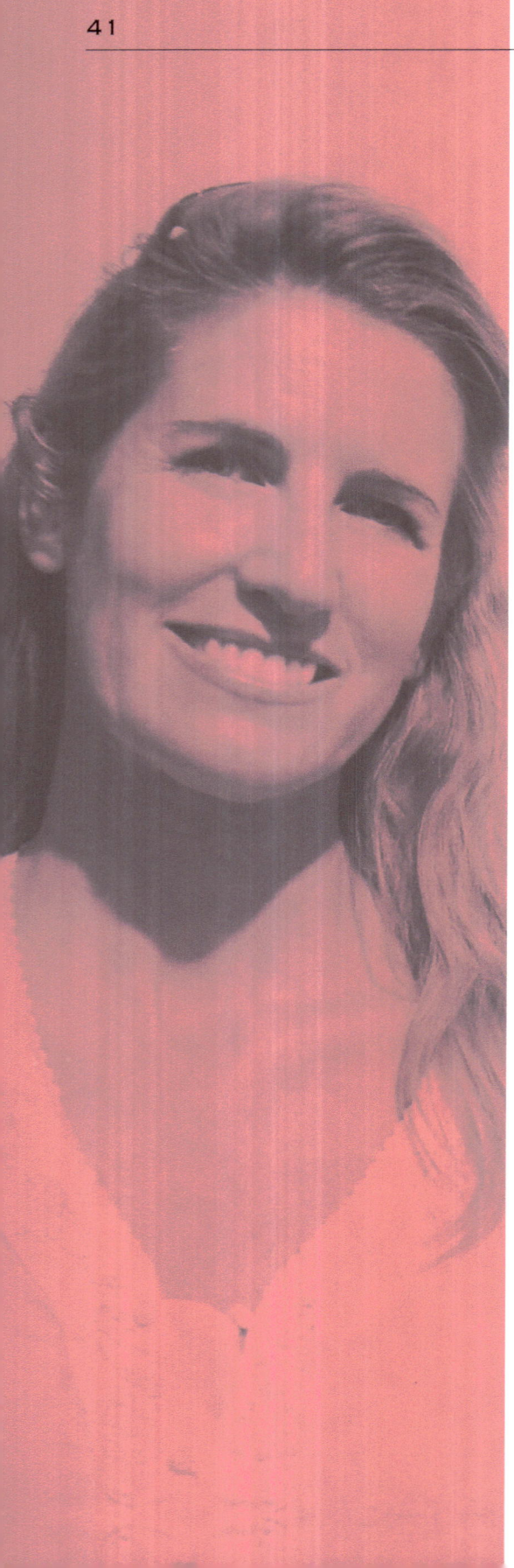

ANDREA KITTS
SENN

I AM A CARPENTER
by Andrea Kitts Senn 2016

We can be feminine,
keep a home and
enjoy delicate crafts,
such as embroidery.
At the same time
we are perfectly capable
of fixing a leak
and swinging a hammer.
In order to build a life
we need a complete
set of skills and tools.

ANDREA KITTS SENN IS A NATIVE OF SWITZERLAND,
HOLDS A BUSINESS DEGREE AND FINDS CREATIVE
REFUGE IN HER STUDIO.
"I'M INSPIRED BY EVERYDAY ITEMS, EXCITING SCI-
ENCE AND DARK SUBJECTS. I COMBINE OPPOSITES,
PLAY WITH SCALE AND LANGUAGE, AND WHENEVER
POSSIBLE, I INJECT A SLICE OF HUMOR INTO MY WORK,
AS WELL AS MY LIFE."

HTTP://WWW.ANDREAKITTS.COM

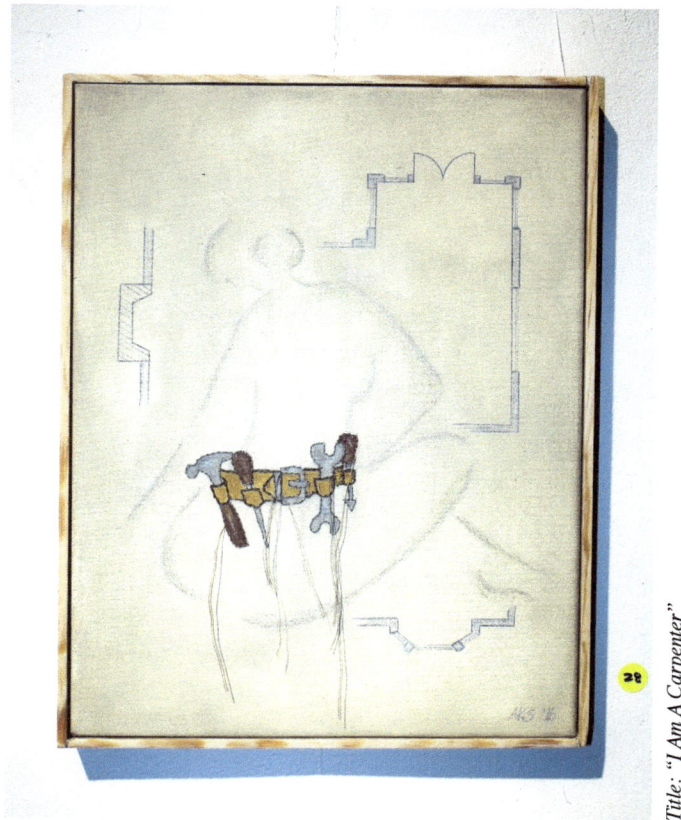

Title: "I Am A Carpenter"
Medium: Acrylic on Canvas, Thread Embroidery, Wooden Frame
Dimensions: 12" x 16" x 1"

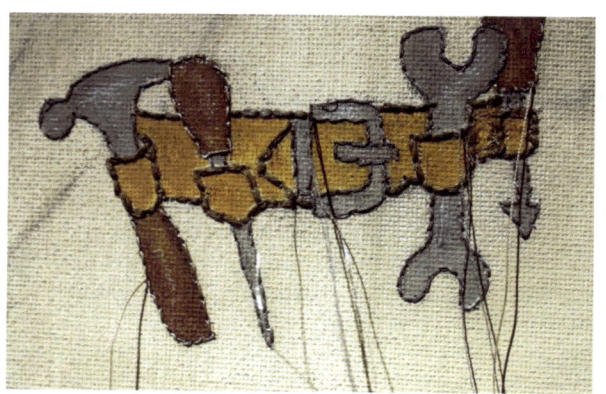

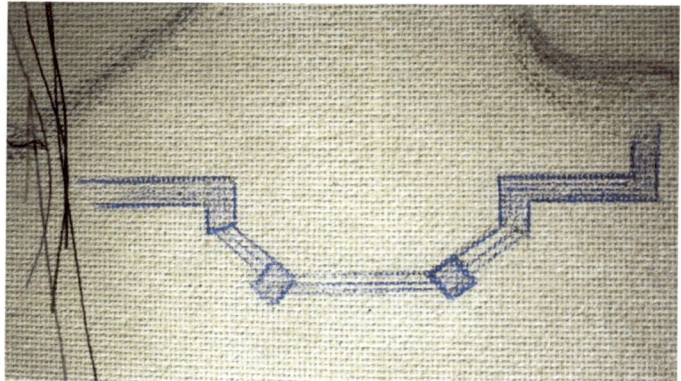

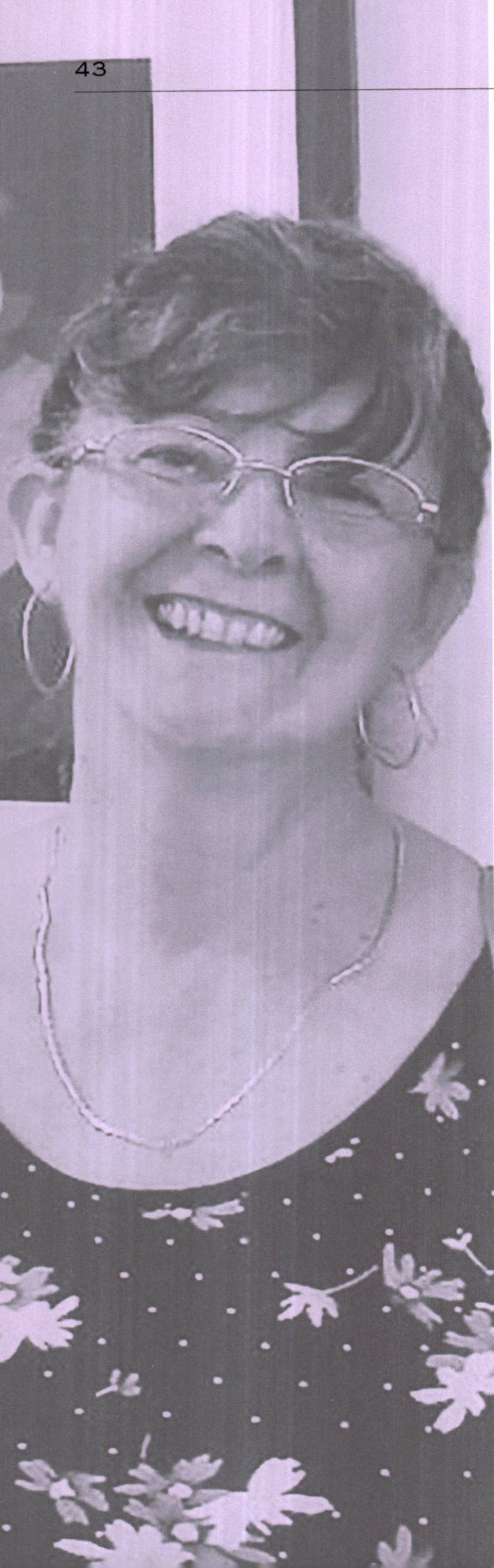

GINGER
VAN HOOK

Experimental Darkroom Photography - "Seeing Double" exposing color negatives upon each other to achieve double exposures during darkroom processing.

"If I were a carpenter, I would build it in color!"

-Ginger

GINGER VAN HOOK WAS BORN IN ROSARIO, ARGEN-TINA, AND GREW UP IN LOS ANGELES, CALIFORNIA. SHE EARNED A BACHELOR OF ARTS IN COMMUNICA-TIONS FROM THE USC ANNENBERG SCHOOL FOR COM-MUNICATIONS AND JOURNALISM, AND HAS A MASTERS IN FINE ARTS DEGREE FROM OTIS COLLEGE OF ART AND DESIGN IN WRITING & PHOTOGRAPHY. SHE ALSO WORKS AS A PHOTOGRAPHER, CURATOR, JOURNALIST AND FICTION WRITER.

HTTP://WWW.GINGERVANHOOK.COM

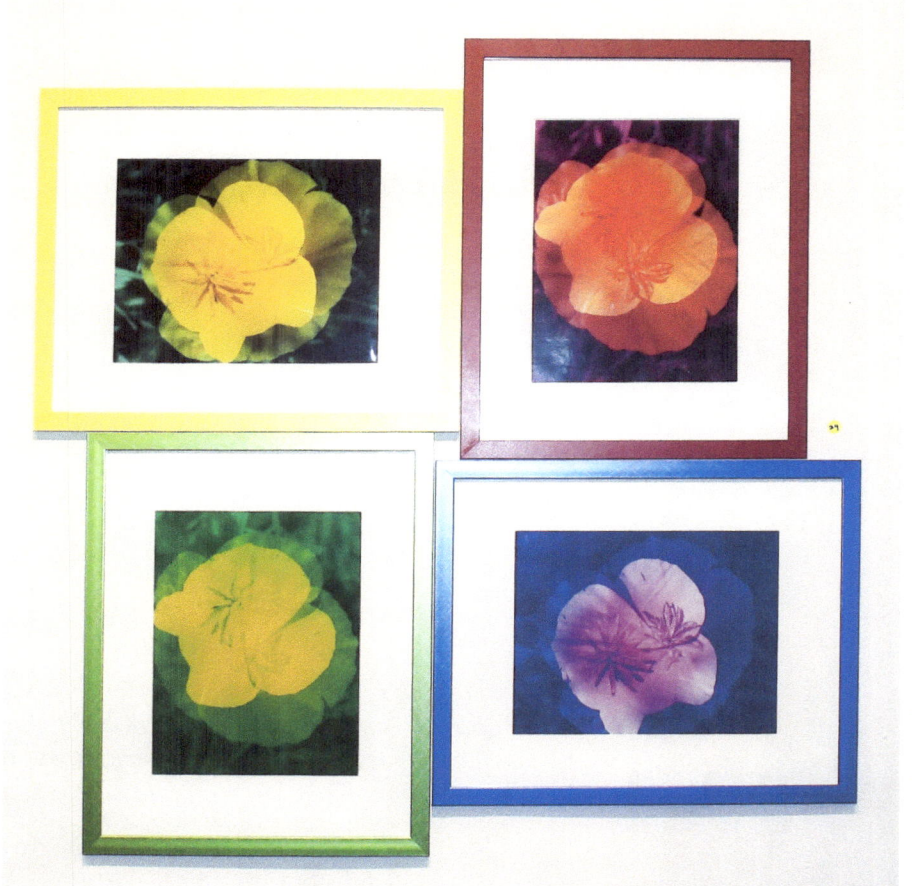

Title: "Seeing Double"
Medium: Photograph (Multiple Exposure via Darkroom Processing)
Dimensions: 16" x 20" each

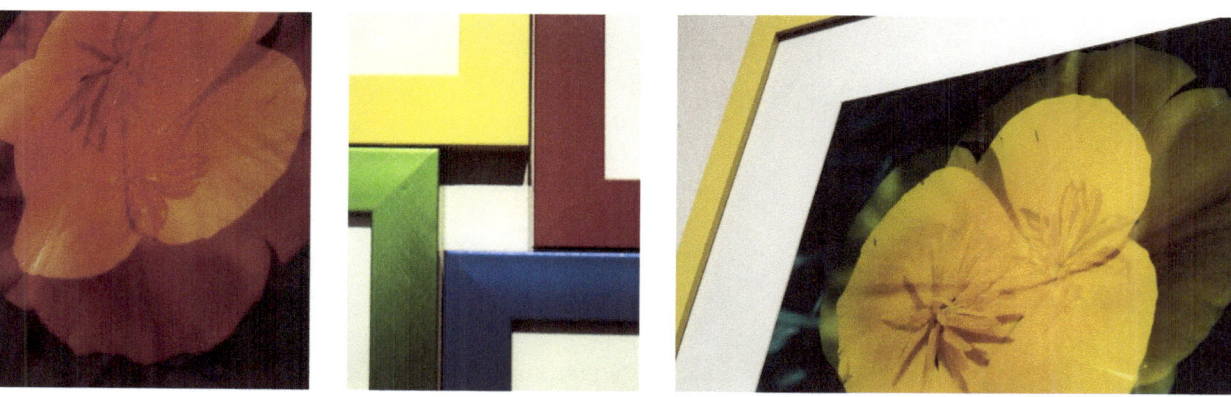

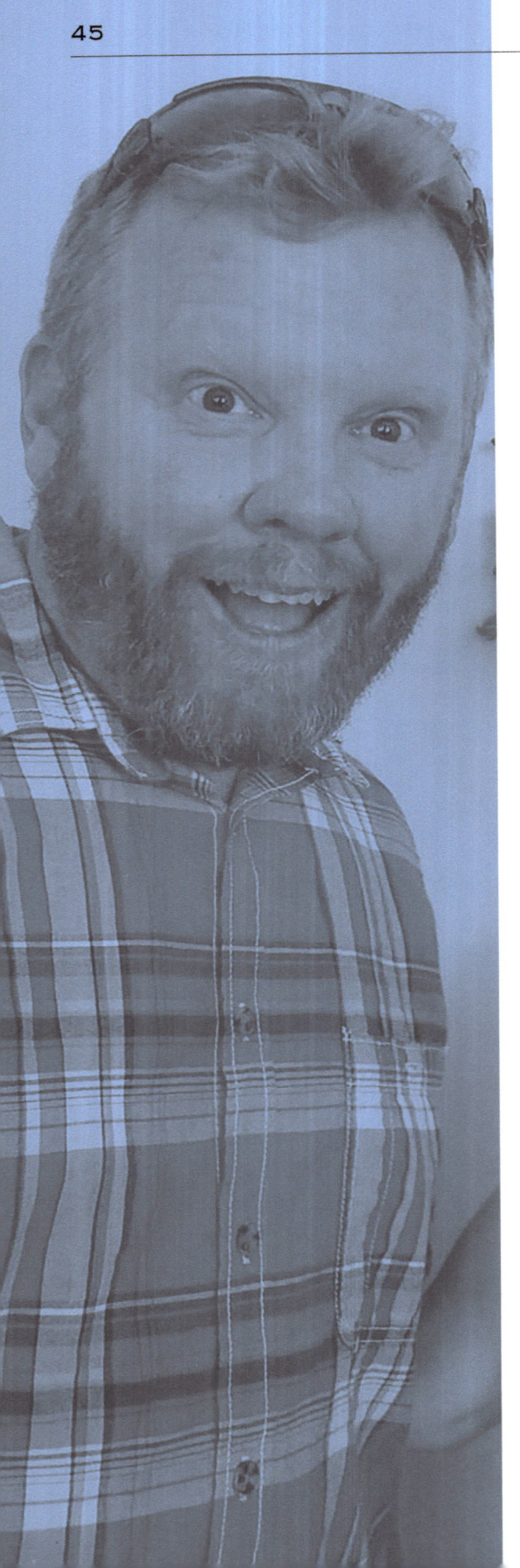

LUKE
VAN HOOK

"I can think of nothing more perfect than the carpenter who built this home using its mouth and force of wing. The humility it displays and industriousness of execution is its signature. This was its future and held its world."

-Luke

LUKE VAN HOOK WAS BORN IN TUREN, INDONESIA. HE LATER RECEIVED HIS BACHELOR OF ARTS DEGREE FROM OTIS COLLEGE OF ART AND DESIGN AND WENT ON TO OPEN HIS STUDIO IN LOS ANGELES, CALIFORNIA.

HTTP://WWW.LUKEVANHOOK.COM

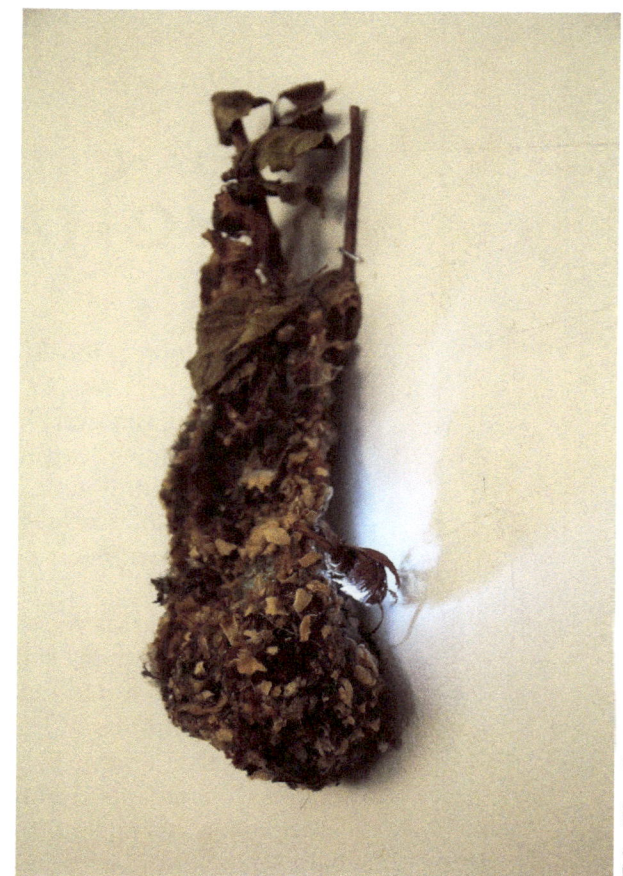

Title: "Home"
Medium: Found Oriole Nest, LED, Battery
Dimensions: 4" x 4" x 10"

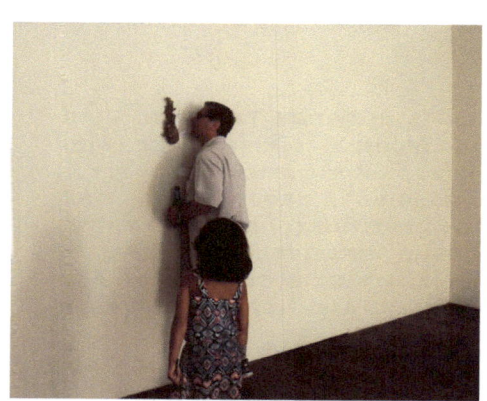
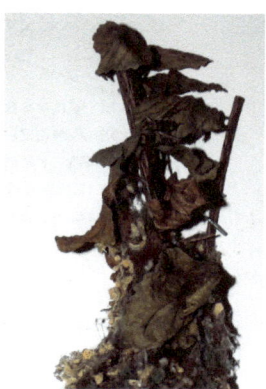
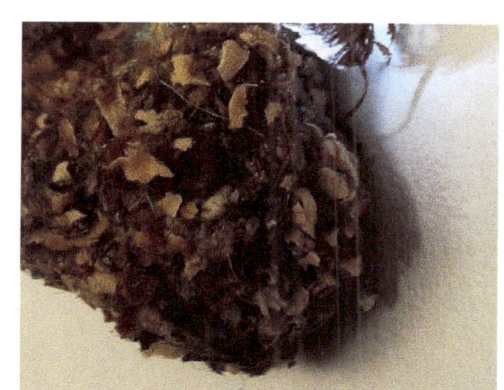

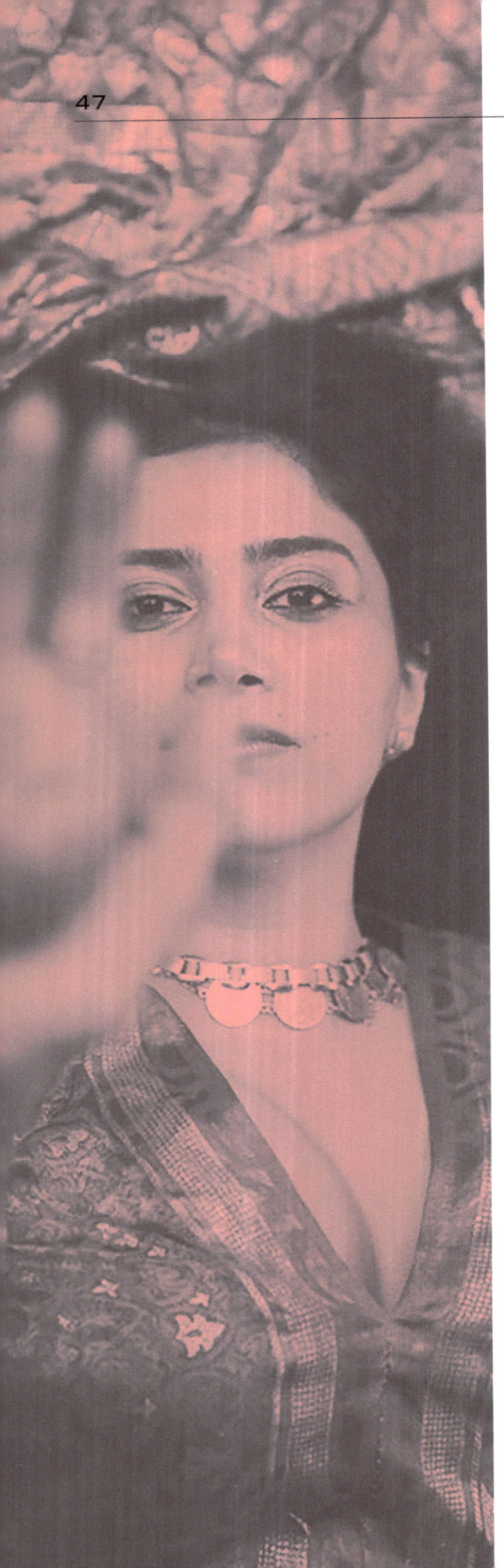

MARJAN
VAYGHAN

"My contribution to the "If I Were A Carpenter" Exhibit, was titled "When I Was A Carpenter" in which I publicly outed footage from over five years of my frame-making practice of sanding, cutting lumber, staining, finishing and working with beautiful pieces of wood which were transformed into archival frames for museums, galleries and private collections.

Most folks who are familiar with my creative practice, are not aware of the many side jobs and gigs I've had over the years. Educator (Teaching farsi, from the age of nine till until I began my MA/PhD studies at UCLA.), Carpenter (at Don Francis Frame Shop in Venice CA, 2010-2015), Designer and Seamstress for most of my life for anyone who asks and is referred to me…. As well as many odd jobs in addition to my pursuit of everything within the creative multiverse.

MARJAN VAYGHAN LIVES BETWEEN TEHERAN, IRAN AND LOS ANGELES, CALIFORNIA. HER PRACTICE IS IN-FORMED BY THIS CONTEXT OF MOVEMENT AND FLEX-IBLE CITIZENSHIP ACROSS BOTH GEOGRAPHICAL AND CULTURAL SPACES, AND THE MULTI-REALITIES THESE SPACES ENGENDER. SHE RECEIVED HER BFA IN SCULPTURE/NEW GENRES AT OTIS COLLEGE OF ART AND DESIGN, LOS ANGELES, AND HER MA IN WORLD ARTS AND CULTURE AT UCLA.

HTTP://MARJANV.COM

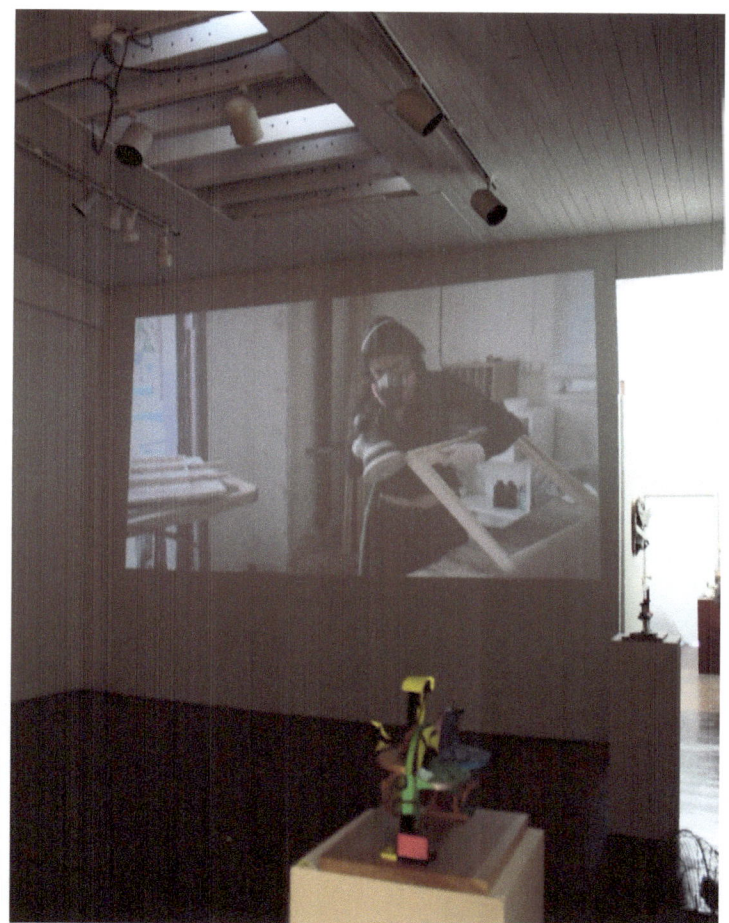

Title: "When I Was A Carpenter"
Medium: Video Installation
Dimensions: N/A

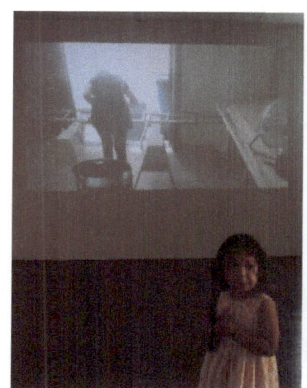 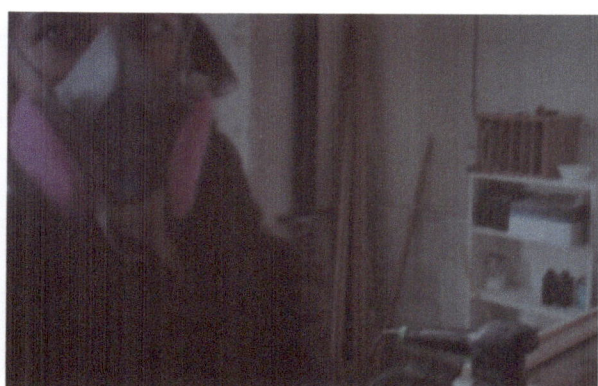 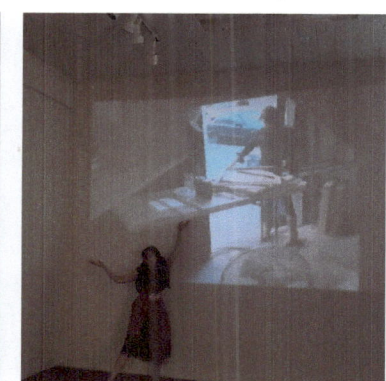

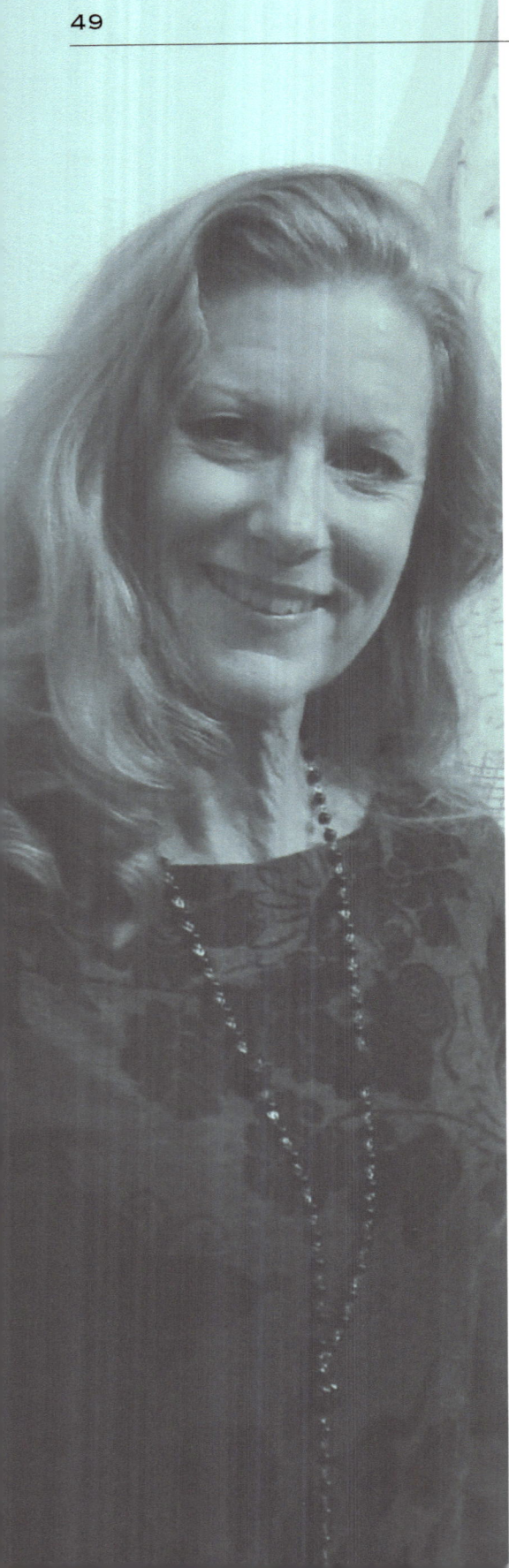

VALERIE
WILCOX

In Valerie Wilcox's "Constructs", her works present a re-imagined understanding of our constructed environment, perceptions of our own identity and how our brain works to piece together diverse constituents.

Wilcox is forming these hybrid constructions using left-over bits and pieces and humble materials that appear as if they were casually cobbled together, off-kilter and with an imperfect resolution. Her constructs can be whimsical, self-reflexive and manage to transcend their base materiality, as her source materials are elevated and imbued with newness of form and function.

VALERIE WILCOX WAS BORN IN SAN DIEGO, CA. AND CURRENTLY LIVES AND WORKS IN LOS ANGELES. ALONG WITH RECEIVING A BFA IN GRAPHIC DESIGN, SHE HAS STUDIED PRINTMAKING, PAINTING, PHOTOGRAPHY AND SCULPTURE.

HTTP://WWW.VALERIEWILCOX.COM

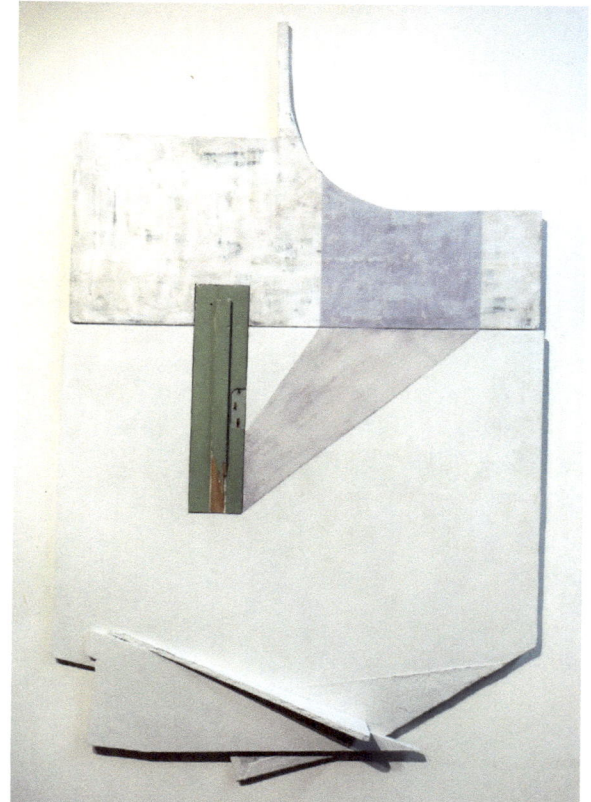

Title: "Passage"
Medium: Mixed Media Wall Sculpture
Dimensions: 66.5" x 41" x 4"

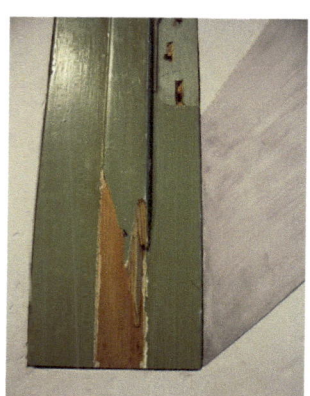

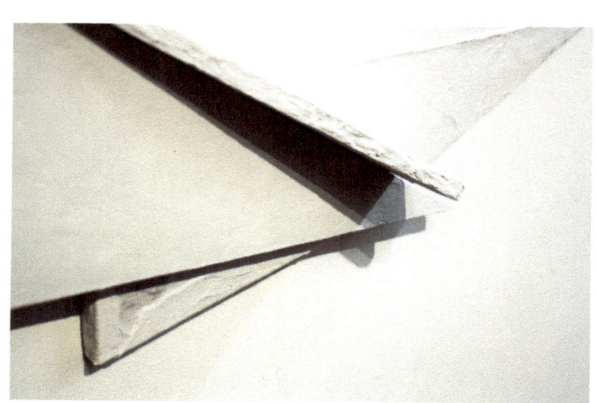

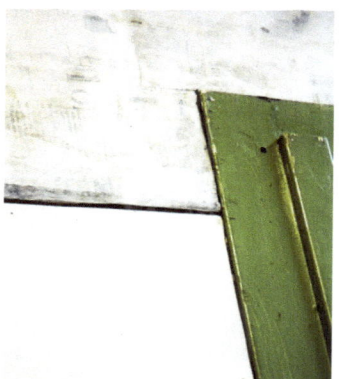

THE SHOW

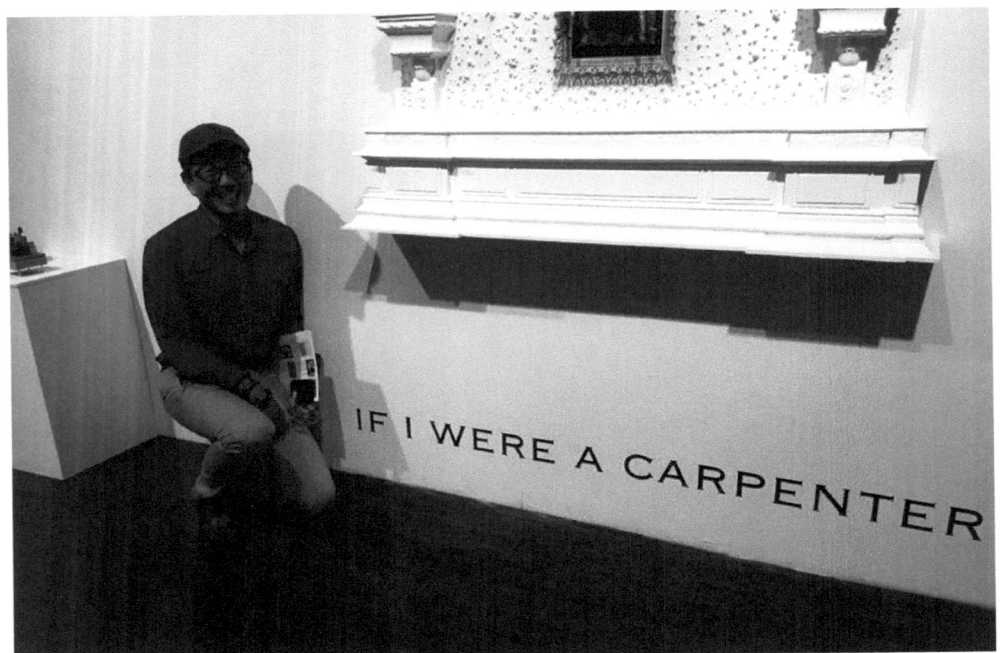

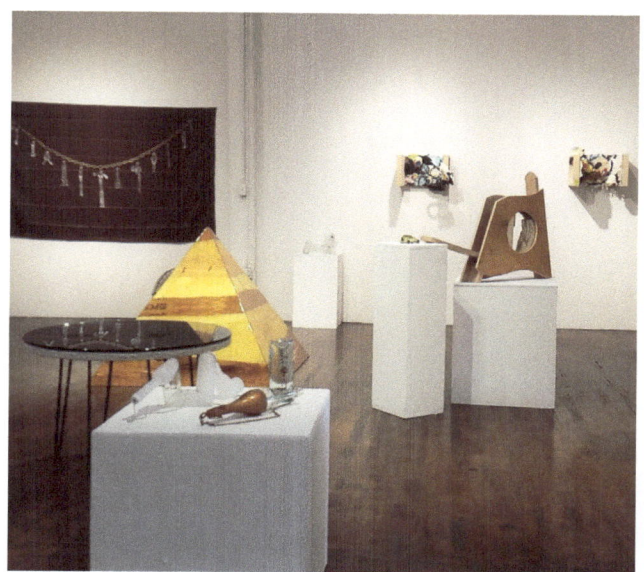 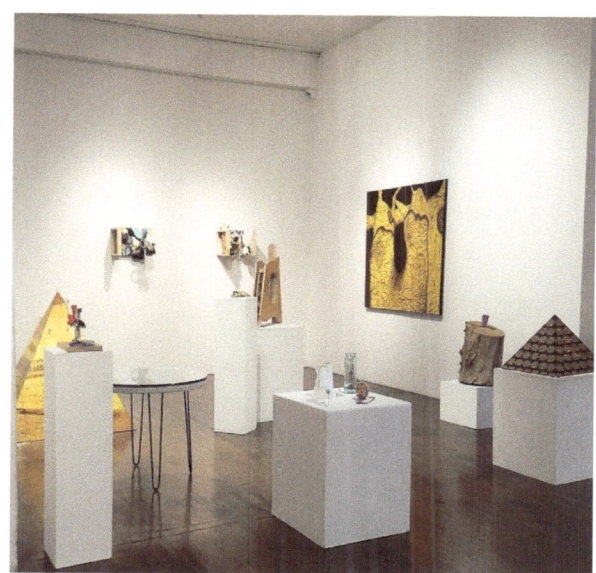

"If I were a carpenter, I would curate an exhibit of works created by my fellow workers-in-wood that were envisioned through an artistic (and not utilitarian) set of optics."

- Steven Fujimoto

"If I were a Carpenter I would create an entire moon inspired kitchen. The cabinet doors would all be moon doors with unique hardware. New stainless steel appliances look stunning and futuristic juxtaposed against the cabinetry and aluminum vent hood that sits over the oven. For the back splash a pattern of black and white Atlas Rocket inspired tiles line the wall. I'd select a marble counter top with speckled grey, black and white stone mixed in for the sink area and work surfaces. Finally the entire kitchen would have special recessed lighting in the ceiling, controlled by individual dimmer switches, to spot and illuminate the moon cabinetry."

Michael Giancristiano

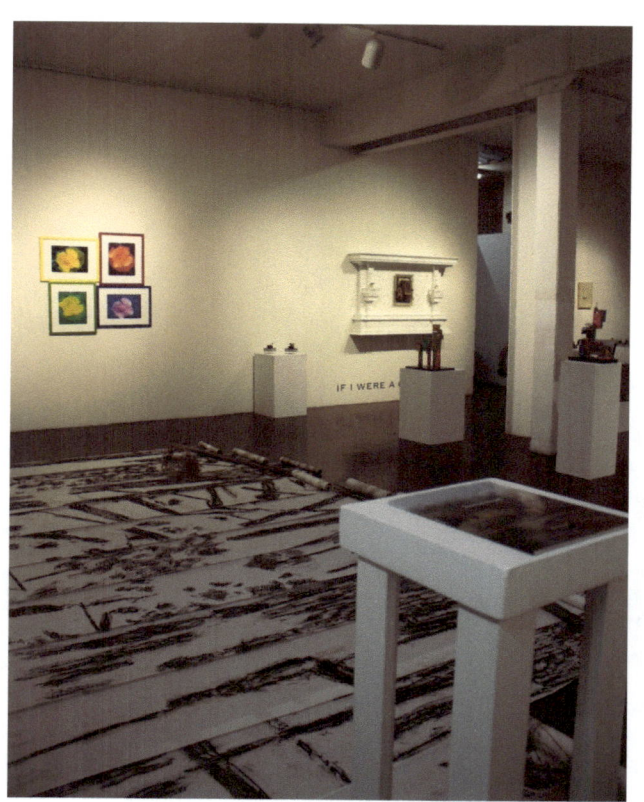

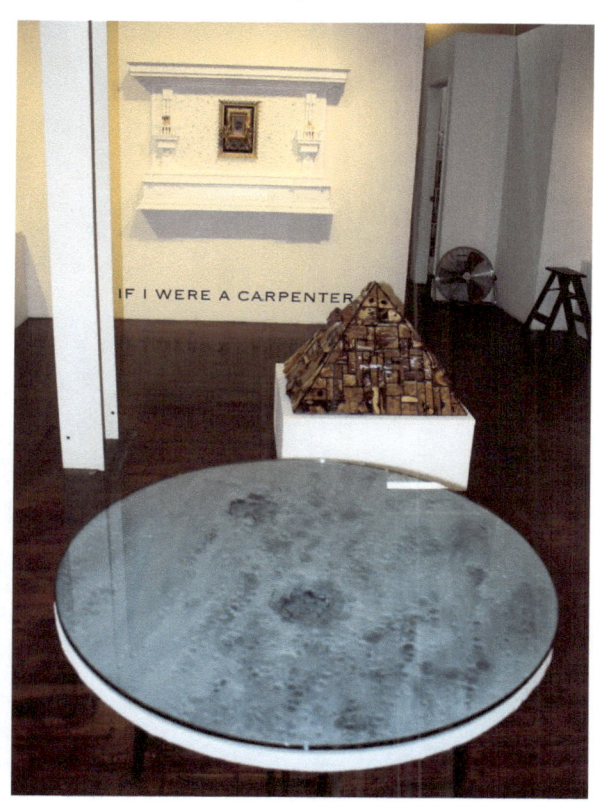

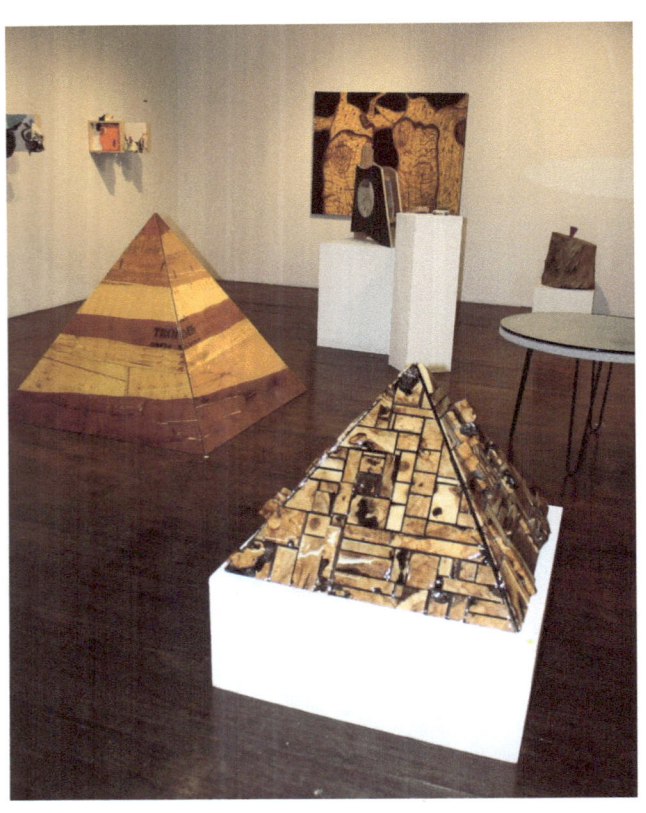

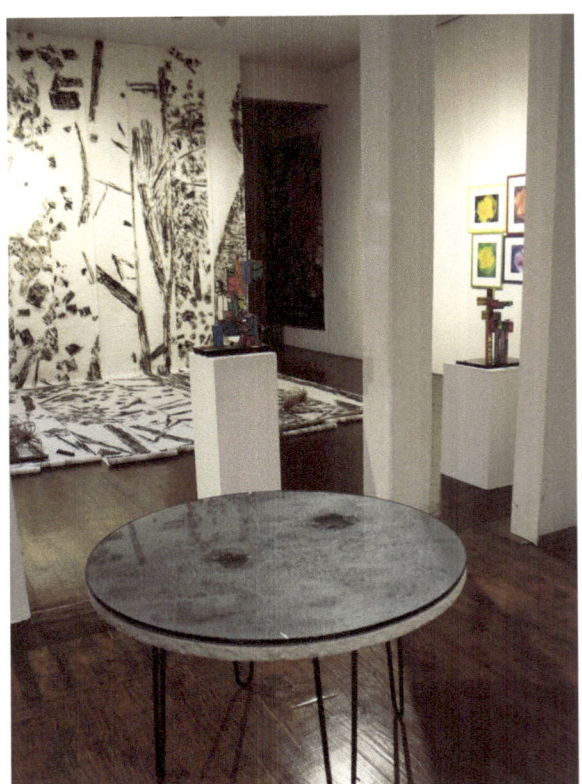

"A young dad that visited the show with his little girl asked a lot of questions about the origin of my piece. As we discussed my statement that women need to be able to take care of themselves to build a life, he paused for a moment and said: Well as a single dad I had to learn how to sew and braid my daughters hair.

The conclusion: in today's world, skills are gender neutral."

- Andrea Kitts Senn

"If I were a carpenter, I would know place with my body. I would touch every bump on a wall and take its imprint with me. Such is memory, longing, loss, and bodily knowledge."

- Flora Kao

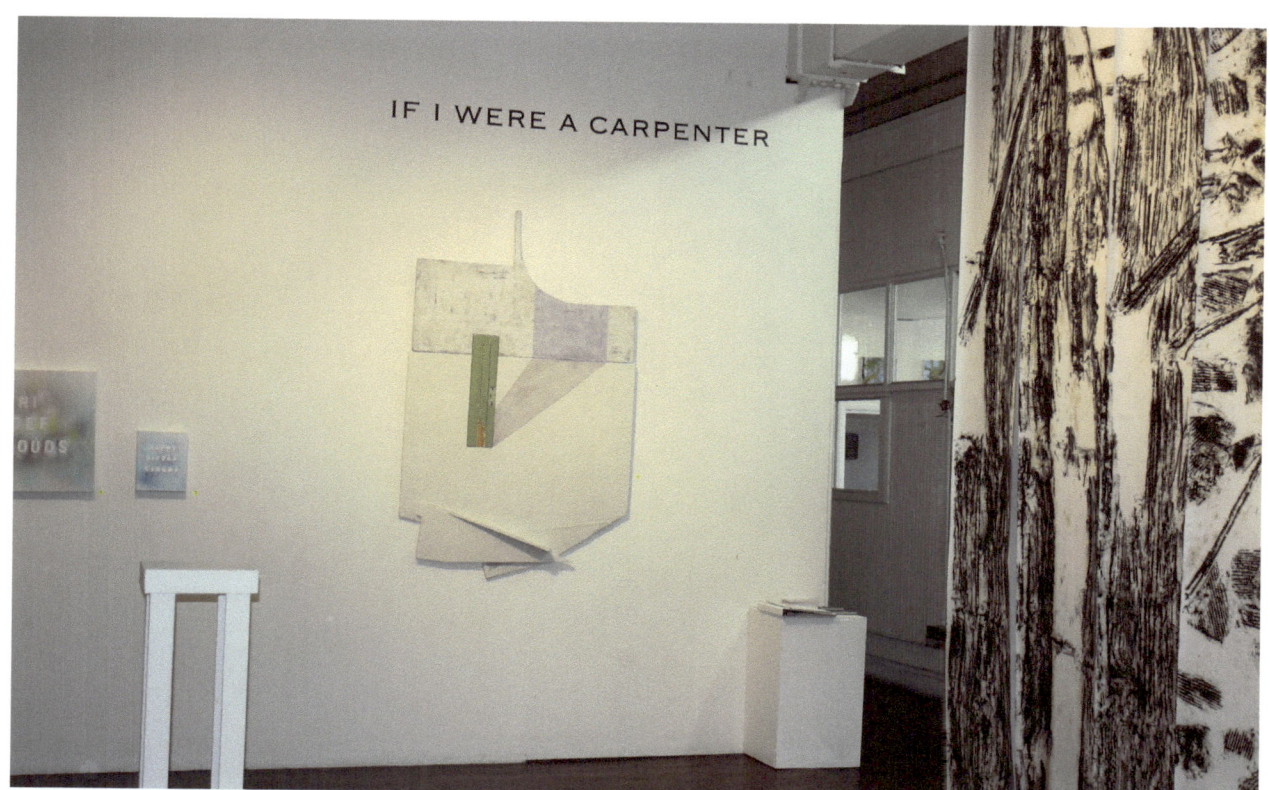

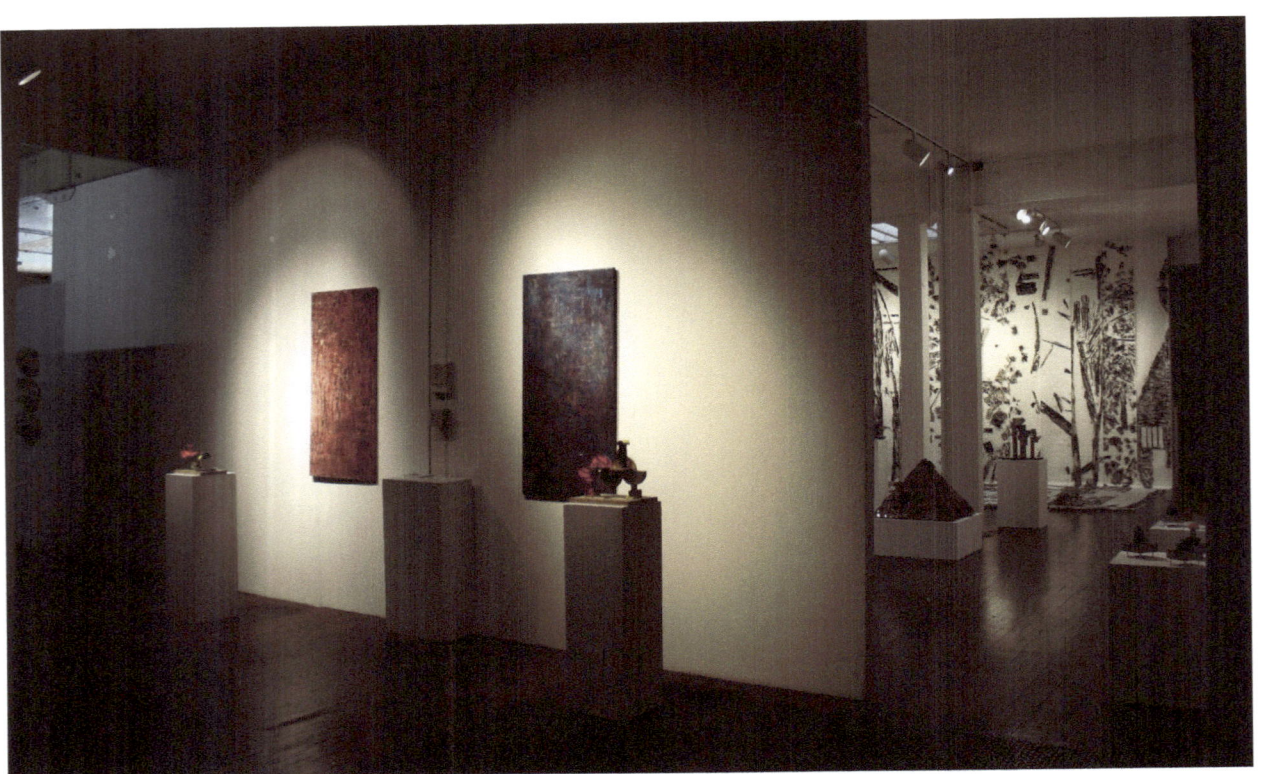

"If I were a carpenter, my goal would be to treat materials, places, and functions with both responsibility and respect to nature which brings awareness to the beauty of the present moment, our delicate relationship to our humanness within nature, and the energies that exists there."

- Ellen Riingen

*By a Carpenter mankind was made, and only
by that carpenter can mankind be remade.*

-Desiderius Erasmus

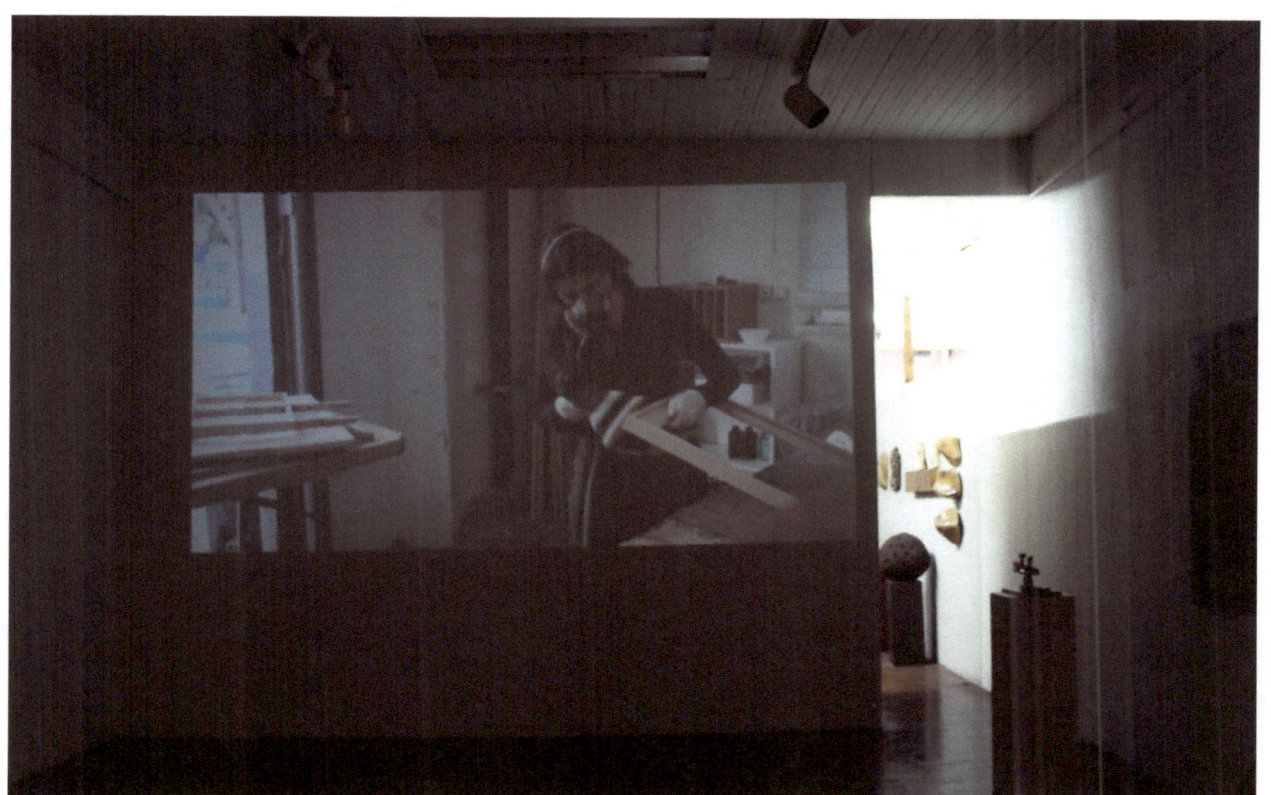

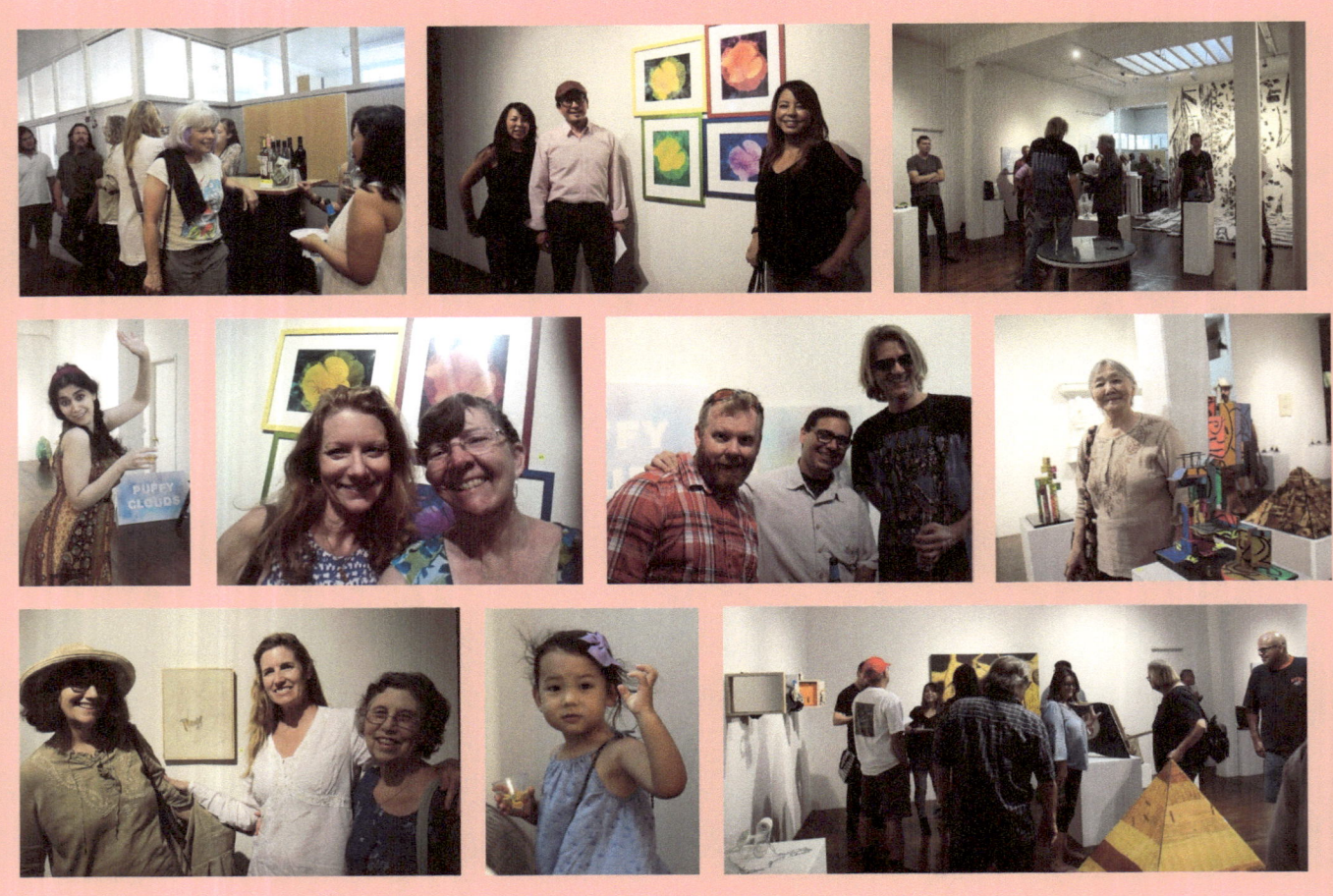

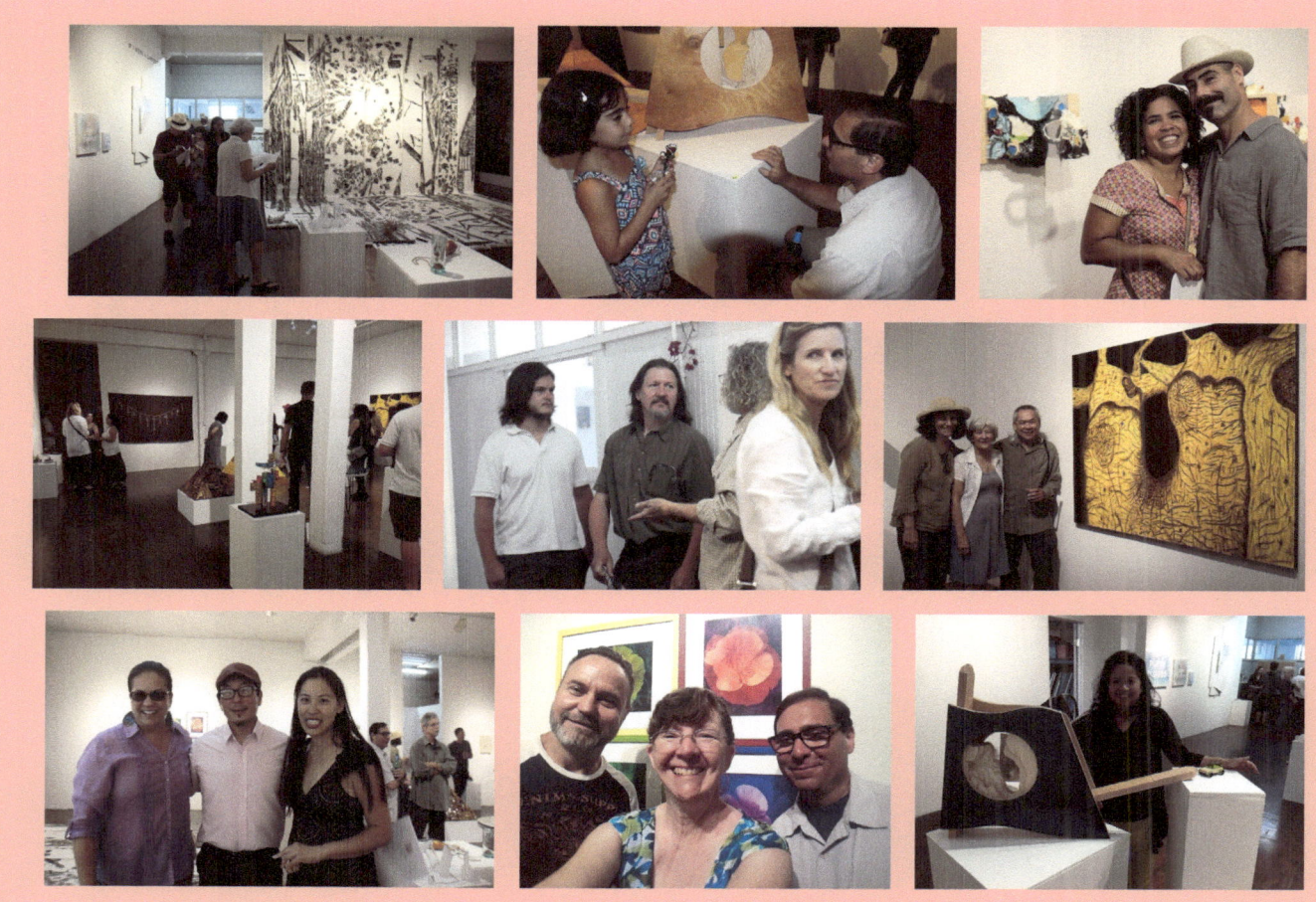

Special thanks to all who support the arts by your attendance, interest, patronage, guidance, and support. We hope we have inspired you to journey into your own making and meaning.
*   - the artists*

www.ingramcontent.com/pod-product-compliance
Lightning Source LLC
Chambersburg PA
CBHW050855180526
45159CB00007B/2686